Christmas 1996.

From Betty coming a close 2nd to Jilly!
x   Love you x   x

D1187169

ENOUGH TO MAKE A CAT LAUGH

DERIC LONGDEN

Enough to Make a Cat Laugh

BCA

LONDON NEW YORK SYDNEY TORONTO

This edition published 1996 by
BCA
by arrangement with Bantam Press
a division of Transworld Publishers

CN 2620

Printed in Great Britain by
Mackays of Chatham PLC, Chatham, Kent

'*There is nothing too little for so little a creature as man. It is by studying little things that we attain the great art of having as little misery and as much happiness as possible.*'

Samuel Johnson

SPRING

CHAPTER ONE

I woke up in the usual way. A cat landed in the pit of my stomach and began pounding, up and down, up and down.

'Not there, Thermal,' I grunted. 'For God's sake.'

He turned round and worked his way up my body, up towards my ribs.

'That's better.'

He moved on, ever upwards, until he was standing with one foot jammed against my Adam's apple, his white furry forehead bopping hard against mine.

'Go away.'

He sat down on my chest and purred. I can do without Thermal first thing in the morning.

* * *

He was lying flat out on my chest, doing his world-famous impression of a very small hearthrug, his chin weighing heavily upon my chin, and with each one of his four paws splayed out as though he had been recently filleted and placed there as a practical joke.

One of his whiskers poked itself right up my left nostril and began to investigate its inner regions. I snorted and the whisker panicked and flirted smartly back in line amongst its colleagues, where it trembled slightly as it told tales of its great adventure.

The bedroom door creaked open and out of the corner of my eye I watched as Aileen crept silently into the room. My wife is registered blind and has to feel her way around. She stopped in her tracks as her hand brushed against something black and hairy lying stretched out on the cane chair.

She knelt down and began to tell the cardigan off in no uncertain manner. 'You're not supposed to be in here, you know.'

The cardigan took not the slightest notice of her. It was a 100 per cent wool cardigan with raglan sleeves and large horn buttons and it wasn't used to being spoken to like that.

'You dribble all over the cushion.'

That cardigan had never dribbled in its life. I could swear to it. I had worn it man and boy for the past ten years, first with pride and then with a growing defiance as it began to look its age. Now I wore it in secret in the garden whenever the evenings grew chilly. But in all that time I had never known it to dribble, not even once.

'Come on, Arthur – get off.'

The cardigan never moved a muscle. I think it was

in shock. The thought of being mistaken for a cat was bad enough. To be mistaken for one of the scruffiest cats in the neighbourhood would form the basis of an impassioned court case at the very least.

Granted it was going a bit thin at the elbows and the horn button with the bit missing was hanging on by a thread and a prayer, but to be mistaken for Arthur – well, the shame of it.

'And it's no good you pretending to be asleep.'

Aileen knelt by the chair so that she could get a good close look at him with her fingertips. Before she picked him up she needed to sort out which was the head and which was the tail. When Arthur arrived on our doorstep he had two broken back legs and a broken tail and we have to handle him with great care.

She patted the cardigan, gently at first, but then with a mounting suspicion as she stroked its woolly back.

It was when her finger got caught in that little tab that you hang it up on the back of the door with that the truth finally dawned. Arthur doesn't have a little tab that you hang him up on the back of the door with, so she rose quickly to her feet, casting an embarrassed glance over her shoulder in case anyone had been watching. She hates being caught out like that.

I hadn't seen a thing. I'd been fast asleep throughout the entire incident and so had Thermal; he'd had his back to the action anyway. So she heaved a small sigh of relief as she slung the indignant cardigan over the arm of the chair and then came over to wake me up.

She sat on the edge of the bed and stroked my hairy chest with a puzzled frown.

'It's Thermal,' I told her, so she scratched the back of his neck and Thermal dug his claws in and purred even louder.

It's hardly worthwhile getting up, I thought. Nothing interesting ever happens in our house.

CHAPTER TWO

Istepped naked from the shower and sneaked a quick glance in the direction of the full-length mirror. It was a big mistake. If I had known I was going to live this long I would have taken better care of myself.

A paw came round the edge of the bathroom door and a small white cat squeezed in through the narrow gap. The cats seem to think I am incapable of going to the bathroom by myself and so they have worked out a rota system.

'He's off again, Tigger – who's on the early shift?'

It was Thermal's turn. It always seems to be Thermal's turn these days. They are short-staffed. Frink isn't really old enough to take her duties seriously and Arthur has gone and fallen in love with a wire brush. A workman turfed it out of the guttering a few weeks ago and it fell into the courtyard and landed flat on its back by the ornamental chimney-pot. Arthur now spends every waking moment out there, sitting adoringly by its side, fluttering his eyelids and worshipping its every bristle.

You can hardly tell them apart unless you look very carefully – the wire brush is the slightly more attractive of the two.

Thermal stood four-square on the bath mat. He's grown into quite a sturdy little fellow and he's very good at being firm.

'Flush the toilet for me.'

'In a minute.'

'Now!'

He can sound very butch when he wants to, so I snapped the handle and the water gushed. Thermal stood on his back legs and poked his head in the bowl. A quick kick up the bum right now would bring me a great deal of satisfaction – never mind saving a fortune on Whiskas.

I reached for the deodorant spray and he was off like a rabbit and down three flights of stairs before I could even press the button. He thinks it's flea powder and he doesn't hang around. He is under the impression that I de-flea my armpits every morning and so far I haven't been able to get my side of the story across to him.

I then spent a couple of minutes trying to decide which was the pair of white pants I had taken off last night and which was the pair of white pants I had just put out for this morning. I must get a system. Eventually I fetched another pair of white pants from the drawer in the bedroom – I am very particular.

Then I spent another couple of minutes trying to decide which was the pair of white pants I had taken off last night, which was the pair of white pants I had put out for this morning and which was the pair of white pants I had just fetched from the drawer in the bedroom. In the end I thought sod it and chucked the lot in the wash basket.

It was going to be one of those days, I could feel it in my water. The phone had rung first thing this morning and Sarah's sweet voice had trilled down the wire. She helps me with the business side of things and I had set a whole day aside for her later in the week.

'I'm sorry. I can't come in on Friday. I'm going on a self-assertiveness training day. I don't want to go, but a friend asked me and you don't like to say no, do you?'

I asked if she had thought of enrolling as a boarder.

We were fresh out of pants in the bedroom drawer, so I had to eeny-meeny-miny-mo my way through the three pairs I had just stuffed in the wash basket. I comforted myself with the thought that the odds were two to one in favour of my picking a clean pair and congratulated myself on the fact that, anyway, it was impossible to tell the difference with the naked eye.

As we ate breakfast the cats began to seep into the kitchen, one by one, from various parts of the house. Tigger would have spent the night on the top shelf of the airing cupboard, and before Thermal staggered into our bedroom to practise his aerobics on my chest he would have had a good eight hours on the fax machine in Aileen's office. There he was able to soak up the gentle heat that permeated through the tiny grilles on top and still be in a prime position to shred any sheet of paper that had the temerity to come poking its nose through in the early hours of the morning.

Frink the kitten slept on the boiler in the cellar. I had converted an old knitted tea cosy into a small bungalow. She would creep in through the handle hole and then snuggle up inside, with one eye peeping out through the spout hole, on the lookout for any intruder who might slip in through the cat flap in the cellar door.

Arthur had lobbied long and hard for the right to sleep by the large radiator in the hall. The other three cats had conceded that right with a smile on their faces – they knew very well that it switched itself off automatically on the stroke of midnight. But Arthur's brain is on a slow burner and he would glow with the pride of victory for the next couple of months or so until the truth dawned on him, by which time, of course, we would be well into the middle of April and it wouldn't really matter any more.

Later I mooched around doing the odd job here and the odd job there. I emptied the waste-paper baskets in both offices and then relined them with a couple of fresh carrier bags from Sainsbury's; the yellowy ones – they're not as strong as those from Marks and Spencer, but they tone in with the decor. Then I sorted out the pedal bin in the kitchen and carted the whole lot out to the dustbin shed. We have three dustbins: one we should have, one the dustbin man left us by mistake, and another that blew in on a high wind one Saturday morning and decided it liked it here.

I pulled them out into the courtyard and they stood

there in a line, blinking at the unaccustomed light.

'You pick 'em up all wrong, you know.'

Our dustbin man creeps up on you without your knowing it.

'Do I?'

'Oh aye. There's an art to it.'

'I suppose there must be.'

'Put your hand there, like that.'

I put my hand there like that.

'Now swing it up and round and over.'

I swung it up and round and over.

'That's it – you've got it. You'll have no trouble with them steps now, you just see. Go on – and I'll bring these here.'

He was right, I had no trouble with the steps whatsoever and I still had one hand free so I could unlatch the gate.

'That's grand that is – we'll make a dustbin man out of you yet.'

I felt rather proud of myself. It probably takes ages to sink in with most people, but I had picked it up just like that. I suppose either you've got it or you haven't. He carried a black plastic bin-liner in either hand and he dropped them both by the side of the wall. A thought hovered for a moment and then tapped me on the shoulder.

'But you don't have to carry the dustbins nowadays, do you?'

'Well, no – not nowadays,' he agreed. 'But we used to have to – in the old days.'

'Then why have I brought this one out here?'

He thought about that for a while.

'I don't know,' he said. 'Is it research? Isn't that what you authors do – research things?'

'Sometimes, yes.'

'That'll be what it is then.'

My right arm had locked solid over my right shoulder and my right shoulder didn't think too much of the idea.

'How do I put it down?'

'Oh it's an art, is that.'

'I can imagine.'

He shook his head sadly as he remembered the old days.

'You see what it was – it was a hold that was designed so as you could throw the bin straight over your shoulder and right into the cart. We used to follow on behind in those days – now the blessed thing comes on after.'

'I see,' I groaned, my knees buckling.

'It's all time and bloody motion these days,' he grumbled as he wandered off down the lane. 'All time and motion and black plastic bags.'

Slowly I sank down onto my haunches and then toppled over onto my bum. I had never realized that being an author was such a heavy lifting job.

The sun poked a hesitant finger over the top of the drystone wall and the little lane celebrated immediately. It was as though someone had just given it a quick flick round with a duster, then hoovered the carpet and hung up a new set of curtains.

I went and sat on the wall opposite. A sparrow with what looked like arthritis came in far too low and made a disastrous landing just short of the dustbin. He was most embarrassed about it. He had a quick look around to see if anyone had been watching and then hopped up onto the handle of the bin and started furking under his wing.

He hadn't seen me, but I had seen him around a few

times before. He was the sort of sparrow who stood out in a crowd, and that's not easy if you are a sparrow – they do tend to look rather alike.

He had one leg longer than the other and he must have bought his feathers wholesale from Oxfam. They didn't fit properly and they needed a damn good press.

I have a soft spot for sparrows. They spend all their lives scratching around for a living, dodging in and out of the traffic just like we do, and by and large they make a very good job of their chosen profession.

Not this one however. He seemed to have no sense of balance whatsoever and, with his head still stuck under his wing, he tipped over and fell off the handle. As he landed, long leg first, short leg second, he tried to pretend that that was what he had meant to do all along. But he wasn't fooling anyone – especially the man sitting on the wall. We had a lot in common, this sparrow and I.

I gave a silent smile and he must have heard me because he turned immediately and saw me for the first time. A rogue feather stood up on the top of his head and for a split second it could have been a very small Tonto standing there before me.

His feather quivered slightly as he took off down the lane, flying at a strategic height designed to frustrate all but the very tallest of cats. He turned right at the waste ground and then disappeared in amongst the bushes. Better keep an eye open – he might be back with the Lone Ranger any minute now.

I lit a cigarette and wandered back into the courtyard. Arthur and the wire brush were curled up by the ornamental chimney-pot, whispering sweet nothings to one another. They clammed up when they saw me coming. I hate it when that happens – you feel excluded and it's very rude. Thermal was nibbling a dry crust on the bird table, but he jumped down and came over, rubbing his rear end up against my ankle.

'*Give us a puff.*'

'You're too young.'

We sat for a while on one of the retired railway sleepers that form a wall around the raised flower-beds. I puffed on my cigarette and Thermal had a good long scratch. It was a pleasant enough way to spend a few spare moments, puffing and scratching together.

It was also very boring. An hour ago my son Nick had flown off to Munich on business and while he was away his wife Lisa was popping over to Bahrain. Annie, my stepdaughter, was already in Chicago for the international book fair and my stepson Paul had gone off on a flying visit to Las Vegas, on behalf of the *Financial Times*.

I was off to Milton Keynes that night to entertain the troops at a sales conference – apparently the company holding the conference do something to sheep that makes them feel an awful lot better and you can't argue with that. All the same I began to wonder where my life had taken a wrong turning.

My world has shrunk. These days it seems to revolve around black hairy cardigans, snowy-white underpants and sparrows who suffer from arthritis and I was just beginning to feel sorry for myself when this Japanese gentleman tapped me on the shoulder.

To say I was startled would be an understatement. Huddersfield isn't exactly a magnet when it comes to

18

Japanese tourists. And of those who do happen to grace us with their presence, very few decide to take a stroll through my back garden at a quarter-past ten on a Wednesday morning. I am sure I would have noticed if they had.

'Mitta Long-one?'

I knew what he was up to. He was selling cameras door-to-door. You could tell. He had an enormous Polaroid and a couple of automatics slung around his shoulders and a video camera hung limply from his wrist.

'Yes.'

He introduced himself. I could be wrong here – my Japanese isn't what it was, but apparently his name was Subaru Mitsubishi and he wanted me to meet his wife Toshiba and their two daughters, Honda and Edna. I had a feeling that Edna might have been adopted.

The ladies were strolling up the path with a hundredweight of back-up stock draped around their necks and then I saw that Honda carried in her hand a copy of *The Cat Who Came In From The Cold* in Japanese.

It's a beautiful little book. I was thrilled to bits when the Japanese publishers sent me a copy. It has a silk bookmark, the oriental script moves in columns, vertically up and down the pages, and you read it from back to front. There is a purple sash wrapped around the cover which, for all I know, is there to tell the would-be book buyers of Tokyo that it's 'reduced to clear' – but I love it.

He introduced me to his family.

'This is Mitta Long-one.'

They each gave me a slight bow and I bent double in return. I overdid it and I thought for a moment that my back had gone.

'And this . . .'

He turned and made an extravagant sweeping gesture with his right arm, his cameras rattling with the excitement of it all.

'. . . this is Mitta Termal.'

Mitta Termal hadn't time to bow. He was sorting out that little bit of fur that always stands up near the base of his tail, the bit he can never do anything with, when the three ladies rushed up to him and he very nearly fell off the sleeper.

I was proud of him. He stood his ground while Honda and Edna photographed him sitting side by side with Mr and Mrs Mitsubishi and only stuck his claws in halfway when Edna sat him on her lap and Honda made him have a good long sniff at the book.

'Smile, Mitta Termal.'

And he did. Most cats don't smile all that easily, but Thermal got the hang of it early on in life. He had wind a lot as a kitten and he's been pretty good at smiling ever since.

They must have taken a hundred photographs. Arthur and the wire brush told them quite clearly that they didn't want any publicity, but the Mitsubishis took little or no notice, so Arthur limped off down to the cellar in a huff. The family then proceeded to photograph the wire brush from all angles, Honda climbing up to the balcony to get an aerial shot while Edna took a close-up, lying flat on her stomach on the stone pavers.

'This is famous Huddersfield wire brush – due to appear in next book.'

Frink made a brief but vivid appearance for the Mitsubishi collection. She flew past at about forty miles an hour, skimming along the coping-stones on top of the high stone wall, with Denton, the wild cat of the north, in murderous pursuit.

Denton isn't the cat he was, not since Arthur sorted him out under the lilac bush last summer. He's ageing fast is Denton, but he can still be pretty dangerous if his intended prey happens to be standing still. Frink stands still an awful lot, but since she can also move from nought to forty miles an hour in one and a half seconds she still takes a bit of catching.

The Mitsubishis were absolutely charming. Aileen came out to see what all the fuss was about and the fuss doubled in intensity. She was photographed with me and with Thermal and with the wire brush and then she invited them all inside for a cup of tea.

I knew that the Japanese had a thing about tea and, as I switched on the kettle, I wondered what sort of ceremony I could conjure up with just a couple of Tetley tea bags and those little packets of sweetener that Aileen had stolen from the Little Chef just out-side Scarborough.

They drank it, God bless them, and Mrs Mitsubishi, or Toshiba as I should call her since we were on first name terms by this time, even had a second cup. I signed the book with some trepidation – I had never done one back to front before – and then they were off. Time was catching up with them.

'And where are you going to next?'

It was Honda who replied – her English being that much better than the rest of the family's.

'We go to Haworth – to see Brontës.'

Eat your heart out, Charlotte. Eat your hearts out, Emily and Anne. The Mitsubishis came here first – to see Mitta Termal and me.

21

It was something to tell the kids when they came back from their separate journeys to the four corners of the earth. We don't have to travel – the world comes here to see us.

I just hope the Brontës were in – they have been known to nip over to Harrogate for the afternoon.

CHAPTER THREE

I stirred the coffee with my fork and then tried to beat some sense into a frozen pat of butter with my knife. The man at the next table glanced across at me. He was stirring a small pot of tea with the wrong end of a soup spoon and he went all embarrassed when I smiled at him, so I pretended I was looking over his shoulder and he relaxed somewhat.

Over his shoulder, and right in my line of fire, stood a large Sikh gentleman and he smiled back at me and then came across and planted himself in front of my table.

'From where do we get the teaspoons from?'

'They haven't got any – they've run out.'

'Bloody hell,' he said in a most wonderful accent

that started somewhere in the Thames Valley and then veered off towards the Punjab via Cardiff and Llandrindod Wells.

'What sort of a bloody country are we coming to?'

I was about to leap to the defence of my beloved realm when I glanced around me. A roped-off section of a motorway service area on the M1 at a quarter-past two in the morning isn't exactly the best starting-off point.

There were about a dozen of us, all seated at separate tables, like long-term prisoners waiting for our wives and husbands to be let in, to visit and bring us news of the outside world.

We were a pretty sad bunch. The scrag-end of the day had caught up with us, leaving us limp and bedraggled with too many miles behind us and still many more yet to come. The shop was shut so there were no newspapers for us to hide behind. We were naked to the world and we hadn't a teaspoon between the lot of us.

My new-found friend placed a pot of coffee on the table, together with a cup and a saucer, and then went off to lodge his tray under a little sign that read, 'Please leave your trays here'. We all stared in admiration – the thought had never occurred to the rest of us.

He was a tall man, beautifully dressed, with an immaculate white turban topping off a suit that would have cost him at least £500 if it had cost him a penny. On one wrist he wore a watch that would have cost him a lot more than the suit and on one finger a ring that had probably already given the watch an inferiority complex.

The blue canvas trainers were a big mistake, however. Through the tattered toe of the left shoe it was possible to glimpse the outline of a red cotton sock and the right shoe took no pride in its appearance whatsoever and was completely without laces.

I couldn't take my eyes off them and, as he sat down, he shrugged and stuck one foot up in the air.

'My shoes were stolen – while I was in the temple.'

We both stared at the big red toe in silence. I don't know what was running through his mind, but I could see a thousand pairs of shoes temporarily abandoned on the temple steps as their owners padded off bare-foot through the large double doors to kneel in worship and pray.

The battered brown boots would be telling a pair of rough rope sandals what a hell of a week they'd just had, while a pair of Barker's best brogues kept them-selves to themselves and tried not to notice the blue canvas trainers that were sweating up on the step below.

The man burst in on my thoughts and sent them spinning off in another direction.

'Often my shoes have been borrowed', he said, 'by people going to the toilet outside.' He flexed his big toe in disgust. 'But never have I had a pair stolen before.'

I should hope not too. It's the sort of thing you might expect from us Christians. Mind you, we wouldn't dream of trusting each other in the first place. If barefoot worship ever enters into our scheme of things then you just watch us – we'll be chaining our shoes to the railings, like mountain bikes or suf-fragettes, and someone will make a fortune out of tiny combination locks that slip in through one lace hole and then out through another.

'There are good and bad in every society,' he mur-mured and I nodded wisely in reply and watched as he bent down and produced a newspaper from his brief-case.

My digestive system doesn't work properly without something to read and for a moment I considered asking him if I could borrow the sports page, but then, as he unfurled it, I could see that the paper was written in Hindi or whatever.

He folded it, first in half and then again, before placing it in front of him, neatly quartered, on the table. Then his hand dived deep into an inside pocket and he brought out the most exquisite fountain-pen I have ever seen in the flesh.

I've seen them advertised in expensive magazines. You look at the pen and then you look at the price and you think – I'd never dare take it out, what if I lost it? He seemed rather overawed by it himself. He weighed it in the palm of his hand, turning it over once or twice, and then like a flash I tuned in to his problem.

No matter how expensive, a fountain-pen just isn't the right tool for a newspaper crossword – the ink runs all over the place. And so I dipped into my own pocket and produced a ballpoint.

'Would you like to borrow mine?'

He smiled and took it from me and in that split second we were brothers, never mind the colour of our skin. He slipped his pen back into his pocket and examined mine very carefully.

It wasn't in the same league as his, strictly second division material I suppose, but all the same I had spent much more than I should have done on it – when my very first book was published and I began to be asked for my autograph.

'Fibre tip?' he asked me.

'Yes.'

'I like fibre tip.'

'So do I.'

'You have more control with a fibre tip than with an ordinary biro.'

'I think so too.'

He admired the heavy tortoiseshell case and took time out to appreciate the fine gold tooling on the clip before he stuck it in his cup and stirred his tea with it.

'Thank you very much – that was very good of you.'

He shook it, wiped it on a napkin and handed it back to me.

'My pleasure,' I said as I popped it back, all warm and sticky, in my inside pocket.

There must be something strange about me, I thought as I continued on the final leg of the journey home. People I have known for only a few minutes seem to treat me as though they have known me all their lives.

My mother was just the same. She once met a woman on a bus – sat beside her for no more than ten minutes and in that time they had arranged to spend a weekend together in the Lake District.

They did too. And they repeated the event once a year for the next six years – Stratford-upon-Avon, Warwick, Broadway and York three times – until one day my mother's friend ran out into the road to avoid some falling masonry whilst on holiday with her family in Lowestoft and was knocked down and killed by an Austin Cambridge saloon car driven by a sales representative who, it transpired, had actually served abroad with her husband in the Second World War.

'It happens a lot more than you'd ever think – that sort of thing,' my mother told me at the time, and I remember, as a young and impressionable child, breaking out into a cold sweat every time I saw an Austin Cambridge or a Morris Oxford come trundling down the street. They looked very much alike and you couldn't be too careful.

My mother had been on my mind during the long drive north, up the M1 from Milton Keynes. The speech had gone quite well. If it hadn't I would have been off like a shot, but I hung around and chatted for a while.

A woman came over to talk to me. She was immaculately dressed and from the amount of deference paid to her by all those around her she was obviously something of a high-flyer. She perched herself on the corner of the table. She had read *Lost For Words* and talked about the time my mother dressed me up as a Brussels sprout.

'My mother was a lot like yours, you know. I won a scholarship to the high school but she couldn't afford to buy me the uniform.'

'That can't have been easy for you.'

'They were very good about it really. A few of the kids tried to make life difficult for me, but on the whole they couldn't have cared less.'

'Your mother would have felt bad about it though.'

'Yes she did. And when the Christmas party came round she was determined that I was going to go all dressed up for once, with a blazer and everything. So she hired the whole uniform for the day – off one of the other kids who happened to be in bed with the chickenpox at the time and couldn't go herself.'

'Just for the Christmas party?'

'Yes. So I turned up in a gymslip and a blazer, with a daft-looking straw hat perched on the back of my head and wearing a shirt that was two sizes too small for me. On the one day of the year when all the other kids were allowed to come to school in whatever the bloody hell they liked.'

As I approached Junction 29 I had an overwhelming desire to go and have a look at the old house where my mother had lived out her last few years. It was after three in the morning, but what the hell, at any other time I would be in too much of a rush. I turned off and made for Chesterfield.

A mile measures only half its length in the early hours of the morning, so it wasn't long before I was parked up in Storrs Road, right outside a front door that looked very much the same as it had done all those years ago. If I closed my eyes I could see her now.

First thing in the morning that door would open just an inch or so. Behind it my mother would have dropped down onto her hands and knees – now she would have slithered down onto her stomach, her chin resting on that little strip of metal that keeps out the draught. Then, from this side, the door would open a little wider and you would see an arm appear, reaching sideways around the corner, feeling for a bottle of green-top milk.

She didn't want anyone to see her, not at that time in the morning – that's what she always said. Other people used to tell me.

'I saw your mother first thing this morning – lying flat on the floor in the hall. Is she all right?'

I would pass this information on to my mother.

'People wonder if you are all right.'

'What people?'

'All the people waiting at the bus-stop right outside your front door.'

'Oh them.'

Her official explanation was that she had two buttons missing from the front of her pink candlewick dressing-gown and she would have hated anybody to see.

'You've been doing it for ages.'

'They've been missing for ages.'

I told her I'd buy her two new buttons, but apparently they were covered buttons, covered in the same candlewick as the dressing-gown, and since that had faded now, two new buttons would have stood out like a couple of sore thumbs.

'Then I'll buy you a new dressing-gown.'

She thought about that for a moment and then came to a decision. 'Oh don't bother. I only ever wear it for getting in the milk.'

One morning she was surprised to see her cat, Candy, sitting by the side of her green-top, waiting patiently to be let in.

She was surprised because, although she was ever-so-slightly eccentric, she certainly wasn't daft, and she knew that a cat who had been run over on the last day of August was hardly likely to be sitting on her doorstep on the 19th of November waiting to be let in. But still . . .

He had much the same markings as Candy and that isn't something you come across all that often.

Candy was a strange-looking cat, sort of a dirty yellow with eyes to match, and he wore a small goatee beard that had been fitted just left of centre. His right eye had a panic-stricken look about it and always seemed to be wondering if it had missed something that the other eye might have seen.

As my mother lay on the floor and stared eyeball to eyeball with this cat, wondering, as you do, whether or not it might possibly be Candy come back as an angel with little wings sprouting out from behind his shoulders, the cat gave a big stretch to ease away the winter frosting on his bum and nonchalantly strode over her right shoulder and into the hall.

He paused as he entered the kitchen to stare into the depths of the fridge she was defrosting at the time. But since she only ever kept a packet of butter, another of lard, half a dozen fish fingers and a small tub of soluble aspirins in there, he quickly lost interest and padded out through the cat flap and off into the garden.

By the time my mother reached the kitchen window the cat had disappeared out of sight and she wondered if she might have imagined the entire episode.

She described him to me in detail the moment I arrived.

'It couldn't have been him, of course, but he was the spitting image. He had a look of your Uncle Frank about him.'

'Was he a bit thinner than Candy?' I asked her.

'I think he was,' she agreed.

'And not quite so well groomed.'

'Now you come to mention it. But how did you know?'

'He's staring in at us through the French windows,' I told her, and he was.

She decided to entice the cat in so that she could have a closer look. Even though her Candy was no longer with us she still fed any number of passing strays. One of them, a sexy little kitten called Samantha who lived in that big house on the corner of Vincent Crescent, called in for breakfast every single morning and more often than not went off with a packed lunch as well.

So she had a fair supply of cat food on the top shelf of the pantry.

She selected a tin, opened it, and planted the contents on a saucer just inside the cat flap in the kitchen door.

'He'll soon smell it and come to investigate,' she assured me, and I settled myself down for a long wait.

'Perhaps he's not interested.'

'He won't be long – mark my words. I have a way with cats.'

I marked her words – she was my mother and it was the least I could do – but the cat didn't seem to realize that she had a way with cats and it just sat there on the patio and examined the loose putty in the French windows.

'He hasn't moved a muscle yet.'

She couldn't understand it.

I made a suggestion. 'Perhaps he doesn't like Ambrosia Creamed Rice.'

My mother put on her reading glasses and then went over and picked up the saucer.

'Why didn't you tell me?' she complained, putting the saucer to one side for her supper and opening another tin: Whiskas lamb and kidney this time.

No sooner had she placed the fresh saucer on the floor than the cat hopped in through the cat flap.

'There you are,' she said. But the cat walked on, straight past the saucer and out into the hall, and stood there waiting to be let out of the front door.

'Have you ever thought that it might simply be using this as a short cut to the allotments?' I asked her as she slid back the security chain.

'His bottom's not as nice as Candy's was,' she murmured wistfully as she watched the cat stroll up the drive.

I couldn't comment on that. I can't remember ever getting a clear look at Candy's bottom. He always seemed to have his head buried in it whenever I called.

Over the next week or so the cat established something of a routine. Every morning it would arrive with the milk at the front door and then, without so much as a by your leave, it would squeeze itself out through the cat flap in the kitchen door and set off down the garden, towards the allotments. Then, somewhere between half-past four and five o'clock in the afternoon, it would appear back through the hedge and complete the journey in reverse.

It quite upset my mother. She was used to establishing, very quickly, a warm and lasting relationship with both human beings and animals, and this, apart from her thirty-odd years with my father, was the first time she seemed to have fallen flat on her face.

'He won't have anything to do with me,' she said. 'I can't get a civil word out of him.'

Secretly I wondered if it might be my father's ghost, come back to haunt us. He used to come in and out of the house with a monotonous regularity. But the cat, as yet, hadn't tried to cut me down to size with some withering remark and my father wouldn't have been able to resist the temptation.

My mother, by now, had moved on to theory number two, the ghostly presence having been abandoned at the first glimpse of that unsightly bum.

'Do you think it could be Candy's brother, come to find him?' she asked.

I told her I didn't think it was likely and at that moment the cat appeared on the kitchen window-sill and began attacking an itchy nipple with a rough little tongue.

'Anyway – if they were related it would be Candy's sister.'

She gave me one of her looks.

'Don't be silly,' she said. 'Candy was a boy.'

Not long after Christmas my mother had to go into hospital for a while and I kept an eye on the house.

One day I popped round to see if everything was still in working order and, as I parked the car, I caught sight of a cat parking itself on a doorstep about four doors down. It was Candy's double and she was sitting by the milk bottles, waiting.

I went over to have a word with her and as I did the front door creaked open and the cat walked straight in. The owner of the house saw me standing by the gate and smiled.

'Hang on a minute. I'll just let her out of the back – I shan't be long.'

I waited and, after I'd brought her up to date with the news of my mother, I asked her about the cat.

'She's a strange one is that. She's the product of a broken home you know.'

'Is she now?'

'Oh yes. They used to live on Heaton Street and then when they were divorced the husband came to live up here with his fancy woman. His wife still lives down there, so every morning the cat goes and spends the day with her, then just before five o'clock she comes all the way back so she can be here when he comes home for his tea.'

'Well I never.'

'It's sad really, isn't it?'

'Very.'

'Mind you – before I found out about it she used to have to walk all the way round, right along Old Road and then down St Thomas's Street. Saves her about a mile cutting through my house, it does, not to mention the traffic.'

The woman was speaking again.

'I had to leave her to her own devices not long ago. I went to stay at my son's for a fortnight, while my daughter-in-law was having a baby. I don't know what the poor little devil did then.'

I did and I told her. She was ever so pleased.

CHAPTER FOUR

Aileen sipped her first cup of tea of the morning, nibbled her toast and marmalade and stared dreamily into space. I tore open a large manila envelope with my bare hands and placed the contents on the business pile.

'Do you want me to read them to you?'

'In a bit,' she said. 'I've just had an idea for the book. Can I borrow your pen?'

I reached in amongst the debris by the hotplate: the contents of my pockets which I had emptied only a few hours earlier.

'Do you want me to go and get your tape recorder?'

'No – this will do. Thank you.'

She began to write in large letters on the back of the manila envelope and then she stopped and examined my biro.

'It's all sticky.'

'Yes. He had three sugars in his coffee.'

'Who did?'

'The Sikh gentleman.'

'What Sikh gentleman?'

'The one who stirred his coffee with my biro.'

She switched her attention from the pen and examined me instead.

'He did what?'

'Never mind – here let me wipe it for you.'

I swished it in the washing-up water and then dried it on a tea towel.

'There you are.'

'Thank you.'

She lowered her chin down onto the table and cupped her left arm around the envelope, so I couldn't copy, and then she began to write once more. After a while she straightened and sighed.

'I've forgotten what it was I was going to make a note of now.'

'I'm sorry.'

'Never mind that,' she said. 'Just sit down and tell me about this biro – slowly, and in English this time.'

The cats were wandering in and out of the kitchen like lost souls. They didn't know whether they were coming or going. I had fed them when I arrived home at half-past four in the morning and their body clocks had gone on the blink.

Aileen pressed the button on her talking watch and the Taiwanese lady who lurks inside immediately sprang to life.

'It's nine-fourteen a.m.'

'Thank you,' said Aileen. She's very polite. And

then, as she trod on the unfortunate Arthur who just happened to be passing by at the time, she wanted to know where Frink had got to.

'She hasn't been up to see me this morning.'

Frink is most definitely Aileen's cat. They spend most of the day together, with Frink draped around the back of Aileen's neck, checking her spelling as she bends her head over the keyboard. Together they make a great team, and first thing every morning the little kitten dashes up from below stairs to sign on.

'I'll go and have a look for her.'

I hadn't fed her earlier on. The others had come nosing around the minute I pushed open the front door, but Frink would have been fast asleep in the cellar and there was no point in disturbing her. She should be more than ready for her breakfast by now.

There are five rooms down there. What once was a kitchen is now a wine cellar – it boasts a huge stone table and is as cold as ice. We have a spare shower room, the only one in Huddersfield with its own coal chute, and it's as warm as toast. There's a room where I keep my books and another in which Aileen's piano takes pride of place.

Frink sleeps in the main cellar. We do all the laundry in there and there's a boiler and a real old-fashioned radiator and it's as hot as hell. Tigger has converted it into a refuge for sick animals and passing strays – that's how we got Arthur.

She came with me now, she likes to keep an eye on things, and she pushed ahead of me as I opened the door.

There was no sign of Frink. She must be fast asleep in her converted tea cosy. I poked my hand in through the handle hole and there, all curled up, was a warm little body, the fur vibrating as the purring reached a crescendo.

'Come on, now – it's time you were up.'

Tigger peered in through the spout hole and it had the most dramatic effect. A startled black bum shot out through the handle hole and lay quivering on top of the boiler. There was something wrong here. Frink is snowy white and has a matching pair of ginger-tipped ears that go extremely well with her little ginger wig.

I pulled out what remained of the kitten and sat it on my hand. It was very smartly turned out; a little black tom-cat, jet black, with a red flea collar, and he certainly wasn't from around here. At least I had never seen him before and neither had Tigger, and she knows them all. Every cat within a radius of one mile has to report to her the moment it moves into the district. She's care in the community on four legs; she's a primary health provider, P.D.S.A liaison officer and Mother Teresa all rolled into one, and she likes to keep her records straight.

She moved in on the kitten and began to administer the first rule in kitten control – that is, give it a good lick all over.

We couldn't find Frink anywhere. She seemed to have disappeared off the face of the earth, or at least that bit of it that butts up to our house.

It was over an hour later that I found her, all alone and forlorn, peeping round the curtains in the shower tray.

'Has it gone?'

Well no, it hadn't. It's not easy to give a small bundle of fur its marching orders, even though he didn't look like a stray – far too smart to have been away from home for very long. I decided to hang onto him until somebody came looking; either that or we found the owner first.

I had snapped the cat flap shut so that he couldn't escape from the cellar, but I changed my thinking on that one after first Thermal, and then Chico Mendes O'Connell from across the lane, seriously risked having their features altered by attempting to pass through a sheet of solid plastic at full tilt.

Strangely enough the other cats didn't seem to take to this one. Arthur hadn't clapped eyes on him yet, but Thermal gave him a very wide berth, and as far as Frink was concerned his name was Damien and he had 666 tattooed on his backside – goodness knows what had gone on in the cellar last night. Even Tigger seemed to have given the kitten up as a bad job, and so I tucked him under my arm and carried him up to my study, where he spent the rest of the morning sitting on the front edge of my printer, going meticulously, line by line, through the outgoings and sundry-expenses section of my tax ledger.

Word eventually reached Arthur that there was a new kitten on the block, so as soon as he had polished off his elevenses he popped up to my office to have a look at him. To be honest I don't think he was all that impressed.

I screwed up an advertising circular that promised to get rid of my cellulite once and for all, and rolled it across the top of the desk. The kitten went berserk. From a standing start he leapt right over my keyboard, landed smack on a payment slip from the Inland Revenue, and then tobogganed straight past the table lamp, before flying off the end of my desk and landing head first in the waste-paper basket.

I fished him out and planted him feet first on the carpet. Arthur shook his head sadly and turned back towards the door.

'When I was a kitten we had to make our own entertainment.'

I worked for a while, but these late nights at long distances are beginning to take it out of me. My eyes began to droop and staring at a computer screen for any length of time doesn't help one little bit.

I had somehow fallen asleep on my left-hand side when I tumbled into bed in the not too early hours of the morning, and I can't sleep on my left-hand side for more than a few minutes at a time.

It goes back a long way – to my childhood. To one night when I was tucked up all nice and cosy in my winceyette pyjamas. My Zorbit towelling nappies were still fluffy and dry and I had my pet pig stuffed under the pillow where I wouldn't have to look at him – his name was Snowball and I hated his guts. My mother always said I would never dream of going anywhere without him.

I *couldn't* go anywhere without him – if I even so much as made a move towards my potty my mother would say, 'Here you are – you've forgotten Snowball,' and she would stuff him under my left arm.

I dragged that bloody pig around with me for years. If I hurled him out of my cot and across the bedroom during the night you could bet your sweet life that my mother would find him almost before he hit the floorboards and I would wake up next morning with him tucked underneath my left arm.

So that night he was jammed face down underneath the pillow, hopefully suffocating to death, when my

41

Aunty May came charging into the bedroom and shook me so hard my teeth fairly rattled.

'Wake up,' she shouted. 'Wake up. Don't you ever go to sleep on your left-hand side. You'll crush your heart if you lie like that.'

And so I can't go to sleep on my left-hand side. I know it's a load of old nonsense, I know it's an old wives' tale, but even so, after no more than a few minutes I can feel the pain in my heart beginning to grow until a rising panic takes over pole position and I throw myself over onto my back once more and take a few deep breaths until my heart tells me not to worry, it's going to pull through – this time anyway, and with no thanks to me.

So I decided to have a five-minute nap in the reclining chair, and when I woke up an hour later the kitten was sitting at my feet. He was trying to tell me something and he had a screwed-up ball of paper in his mouth.

'Do you want me to throw it for you?'

I tossed the ball across the room and he scampered after it and brought it back to me.

Thermal would have killed it. Frink would have chased it until the ball of paper was totally exhausted. Tigger would have put a plaster on it and kissed it better and Arthur would have had nothing to do with it whatsoever because it was the wrong shape (Arthur dreamed of playing rugby league for Wigan).

But this kitten seemed to think he was a puppy. Every time I threw it he brought it back.

Aileen pushed open the door and came in, sinking down into the easy chair. I took the kitten over to see her and he dropped the ball of paper in her lap.

'If you throw it, he'll fetch it for you.'

She threw it and he fetched it, a dozen times, each time jumping up onto her knee.

'He's lovely. Do you think Tigger found him?'

'No – not this time.'

She stood up, the kitten draped over her shoulder.

'Come on then, with me. Let's find you something to eat. You mustn't disturb Deric, he's working hard.'

Being married to a blind wife does have its advantages. Whenever a guilty look creeps across your face, it can get all the way to the other side without being found out.

Over the next twenty-four hours Aileen and the kitten developed into a highly polished double act.

From her desk she threw little balls of paper for him and he brought them back to her. In the kitchen she placed a paracetamol tablet by the side of her plate and by the time she had screwed the lid back on the bottle and closed the cupboard door the kitten had gone and dropped it on her foot.

He sat close by her on the dressing-table and then, having already perfected the art in my office, he dived two and a half feet into the waste-paper basket to recover her discarded cotton-wool balls.

He even tried to put her ear-rings back in the drawer after she'd already threaded them through her lobes, but he gave that one up as a bad job the moment she started screaming.

'He's a grand little chap, but he's a bit wearing.'

Frink has a variety of talents. She's a trained juggler, a karate expert and a con man, all rolled into one. She can walk on her back legs and climb drainpipes and she has a great sense of humour. But above all she has affection dripping out of every paw; she loves everyone and everything; she loves flowers and she loves mice. But above all she loves Aileen and she was getting as jealous as hell.

This little black kitten had eyes for no-one. He was only interested in the latest screwed-up piece of paper, paracetamol tablet or cotton-wool ball. Like a Member of Parliament's his eyes went straight through you, working the room, ever on the lookout for the more rewarding option. And so it wasn't too much of a disappointment that night when I spotted an advertisement on the back page of the *Huddersfield Examiner*.

Lost. Small black kitten in the Greenhead Park area last Wednesday morning. Reward, ring 01562 . . .

I rang that evening and the voice on the other end of the phone had been born and bred in Yorkshire, as had his father's voice and his father's voice before him.

'Well I hope it's 'im – wife's been goin' barmy.'

I grabbed hold of the kitten as he passed by me on his way to fetch yet another cigarette butt out of the ashtray, and then held him upside down as I examined his undercarriage for distinguishing marks.

'He's got a very small patch of grey under his chin.'

The man sounded doubtful.

'I don't think so – not that I remember.'

Apart from that he was just another black kitten.

'He's got green eyes.'

'Can't say I ever noticed, but he were a pain in the arse.'

Now we were getting somewhere.

'What did he do if you threw a ball of paper for him?'

I heard the voice break into a smile and knew that we had cracked it.

'He'd go and fetch it for you. He'd fetch anything, just like a dog would. That's why we called him Curtly.'

I didn't quite get that.

'After a dog we used to have.'

'Oh, I see. I think you had better come and get him then.'

Apparently that wasn't as easy as it sounded – not until the weekend.

'Well, I could bring him over to you.' I had another look at the advert. 'Where exactly is 01562?'

'Kenilworth.'

I looked at the kitten with a new-found respect. He couldn't have walked, surely, and he was too young to drive. It was well over a hundred miles.

'We've only been down here a few days. He jumped out of the removal van as we were going past Greenhead Park.'

It was then that I had my bright idea.

'Look, I'm off down to London on Saturday. How about meeting me somewhere on the M1 – say Leicester Forest East, about eleven o'clock.'

He thought that was very good of me and I was only too pleased he was prepared to have the damn thing back.

'You'll recognize me,' I told him, 'I shall be standing in the main entrance hall with a small black kitten under my left arm.'

'And you'll recognize me,' he said, 'I'll be wearing blue jeans and a baseball cap and I'm the same colour as the kitten.'

CHAPTER FIVE

Within minutes of hitting the M1, Aileen was fast asleep. She can just make out the flashing of lights and she can hear the whoosh of speeding cars all around her and that's about all. So she escapes from this nightmare world by simply dropping off to sleep – I think it's a wonderful facility.

On winding country roads she can see virtually nothing at all. She can't see the corners coming. It's like being blindfold on a roller-coaster – just imagine it. And so once again she drops off to sleep. She's great company. But I don't mind really. As my brain steers the car down the fast lane, my mind goes walkabout on the hard shoulder and plays nicely with random thoughts. Like how come it says 'locally produced eggs' on the back of that articulated lorry? How far

can an egg travel before it ceases to be locally produced? No more than a few miles surely. So why do
they need a lorry that size? Any moment now the
driver will slam on his brakes as he realizes his mistake.

'Oops – I've overshot.'

A lad on a bike could deliver locally produced eggs,
or let's say a small van if you are in a really big way.
Maybe I'm doing the firm an injustice. Perhaps the
lorry is stuffed full of hens, all hanging on like mad
because they've been told not to lay so much as a roll
of lino until they reach Colchester.

'OK, girls – we're here now. Bombs away.'

Or do you think someone is trying to pull the wool
over our eyes?

For the first time since I reversed him out of the tea
cosy the little black kitten was being as good as gold.
The other cats had become thoroughly fed up with
him by the time we bundled him into the car.

He had wanted their food – not his own. He went
from saucer to saucer, muscling in until they pushed
off and left him to it. Then he didn't want it anymore.

He wanted to sit where they were sitting, on the
same bit of carpet or on the same spot on the same
arm of the same chair. They were remarkably patient
with him and he got away with it until he made the
mistake of trying to make a date with Arthur's wire
brush. If I remember rightly he had completed four
somersaults and a sort of a half-hearted crossover and
triple-flip before the ornamental chimney-pot
stopped him dead in his tracks.

You would have thought he'd have had the sense to
keep out of Arthur's way after that, but we are talking
about a driven kitten here. I have a mental image of
him with all four legs wrapped around the scratching

post, clinging there for almost half an hour, just so the other cats couldn't get at it.

'*It's mine – all mine.*'

Tigger left him to it. '*Just ignore him.*'

Thermal tried to explain that it was his scratching post. '*I think I've got the receipt somewhere.*'

But Arthur didn't even seem to see the kitten. He just strolled up and had a good scratch, and when he left there was a corrugated kitten lying in a crumpled heap on the floor.

Usually, when we go away for the weekend, the cats re-enact the death scene from *Camille*. Tigger is sure she has a touch of the flu coming on and Thermal's leg begins to play him up again – it's bound to be thrombosis this time.

Frink has no idea what's going on, but Arthur is getting the hang of it. His lugubrious look has to be seen to be believed and he has recently mastered the fine art of moulting on demand.

This time, however, they seemed to know that we were packing the kitten as well as the suitcases and they couldn't wait to see the back of us. Thermal even helped me compose a note for Bridie.

Dear Bridie,

Thank you for looking after the cats once again. Just one or two reminders. Arthur's gone off his tuna. I have put a tin of sardines in tomato sauce on his pile, just as a special treat. If you give him too much he'll go off it.

Thermal slapped his bum up against my arm.

'*Don't forget to tell her about my tablets.*'

'Shut up – I'm thinking.'

Please remember to feed Frink up on the work surface, just round the back of the kettle. If you feed her on the floor with the others, Thermal eats it.

'*I never.*'
'I've seen you.'

And another thing. Tigger and Thermal like Whiskas Crunch with their coley, but Arthur doesn't. He likes the big biscuity things on their own, the fish flavour – not the meat.

'*Tell her lots of Whiskas Crunch.*'
'Shut up.'
'*And don't forget my tablets.*'

There are two sorts of tuna. Tigger and Thermal like the one in brine, but Frink will only eat the tuna in water. Arthur's gone off tuna altogether.

'*You've told her that already.*'
'Shut up.'

The coley steaks take just two and a half minutes in the microwave and there's some leftover chicken in the fridge – they can have that.

'*Is it garlic chicken?*'
'Yes.'
'*Good.*'

I've put their tins in separate piles, with their names on a piece of paper. You'll find a bottle of Brewer's yeast tablets behind Thermal's pile. He has one first thing in the morning.

'And another at night.'

And another at night – if he's behaved himself.

The more I wrote the more of an idiot I felt. I couldn't bring myself to tell Bridie that I always added a drop of hot water to Tigger's milk and that she likes her fish chopped up into little bits, whereas Arthur prefers to tear his apart with his bare paws.

Bridie's cat, Chico Mendes O'Connell, will eat anything. Mashed potatoes, corn on the cob, vole on the hoof – anything. Bridie has brought him up properly and she was bound to think that I was stupid.

Although, now I come to think of it, when Bridie popped over to Ireland for a few days it took Aileen and me, all six of Bridie's grown-up kids, their wives, husbands and lovers and a feint-ruled exercise book from W. H. Smith to cope with his comings and goings. I have it still.

6.35 Monday. Popped in – fed Chico.

Paul

Didn't know whether that was a.m. or p.m. – so fed him again at 7 p.m. Monday. He was hungry – must have been a.m. Chico says nobody asked him if he wanted to go on holiday or not.

Deric

Fed Chico at 9 a.m. Tuesday. He stayed in. John would be happy to have him stay in Wakefield – but would he come?

Breda

Dear Breda. Have asked Chico about Wakefield

50

and he can't make up his mind. Fed him at 5 p.m. Tuesday. Chico says what about traveller's cheques?

Deric

Let Chico out 9.45 p.m. Tuesday. Had to wake him first.

Aileen

9.45 p.m. Tuesday. That woman from across the lane came and woke me up, bold as brass.

Chico

Oops! Let him in again, 9.55 p.m. Tuesday. Fed him and now he's upstairs fast asleep. I tell a lie – he's just gone out again.

Simon

I don't know whether I'm coming or going.

Chico

Lunchtime Wednesday. Fed Chico and ourselves. He is now upstairs having his siesta.

Breda, Claire and little John

5.30 p.m. Wednesday. Just topped him up. Brought him a video from the shop. Tomorrow I am taking him to have his hair done. PS – Who the hell is Little John?

Deric

Who the hell is Chico?

Big John

10.00 p.m. Wednesday. Chico nowhere to be seen. Brought a bottle of wine over and shared it with

Simon while we waited. 11.45 p.m. Wednesday. Let Simon out – I think he's on heat.

Deric

9.00 a.m. Thursday. Chico finally arrived home. Said he'd missed the last bus from Brighouse. He had a shower and went to bed.

Simon

9.25 a.m. Thursday. Fed Chico and then read Simon's note. Sorry.

Chris and Helen

9.45 a.m. Thursday. Fed Chico and then read Chris and Helen's note. Sorry.

Margaret, David, Helen and Gregory

11.15 a.m. Thursday. There's something sticky on the kitchen floor. I think Chico has exploded.

Aileen

5.15 p.m. Thursday. Remind me – what colour is Chico? I think I have been feeding the wrong cat.

Paul

10.05 p.m. Thursday. May I take this opportunity to wish a Merry Christmas to all our readers.

Chico

9.35 a.m. Friday. Fed Chico. Can somebody tell me when Bridie is coming back? I can't take much more of this. I let Chico out.

Deric

12.15 a.m. Friday. Chico was upstairs. I think he has

his own key. Bridie was due back half an hour ago.

Helen

2.25 p.m. Friday. Sorry I'm late. I do hope Chico hasn't been any trouble.

Bridie

If there is a more obvious way of making a fool of yourself than writing a note for the cat-sitter, then it must be standing in the entrance of a motorway service station for any length of time with a little black kitten under your arm.

His owner was already half an hour late and so many of those people who had patted him on their way in for a meal were now patting him on their way out. Some brought him scraps of food from their plate.

'Would he like a sausage?'

'He's had three already.'

And they had gone in the bin. He wasn't in the mood for eating – he was totally overawed by the occasion, just as he had been on the drive down. He sat on the parcel shelf, gawping at the traffic like a nodding-head Alsatian, and for once in his short life he had been a pleasure to have around.

'Will he eat a scone?'

'Yes, of course he will. Mind you he'd much prefer a nice gooey profiterole or, better still, perhaps you wouldn't mind popping back to see if you can find him a thick slice of toast and marmalade.'

I didn't really say that, but some of the offers bordered on the ridiculous. Who in their right mind would offer a cat an egg and cress sandwich?

While the catering corps drifted past me on their way out I kept an eye on the vast army of car-parkers who were pushing their way in. He was nearly an hour late now and I was trying to come to terms with the fact that I might be walking round London this weekend with a kitten stuck underneath my arm.

Never mind what he was wearing, every time I saw a black face in the crowd I smiled brightly and moved in close. Perhaps he'd forgotten about the baseball cap and the jeans, maybe they were in the wash.

'Stick close to me, honey – I think he's a homosexual.'

I blame the red flea collar. It made us look a right pair. I went to collect Aileen from the cafeteria so that she could balance up the act.

She had over-dosed on coffee and was only too glad of the chance to make her escape and as we sailed through the automatic doors I saw him, racing across the car park in his baseball cap and jeans.

'I'm ever so sorry – I couldn't get the car started.'

'That's all right.'

He took the kitten from me and gave it a big cuddle.

'Do I owe you anything – food, petrol?'

'Course not.'

'That's very nice of you.'

We stood there, all three of us, beaming like idiots – the way you do.

'I'd better be going – had to leave the car running. Daren't switch the engine off.'

He turned to go and then stopped by the RAC caravan.

'Kids will be chuffed to death. The dog'll leave home again, but the kids'll be thrilled to bits.'

Aileen and I strolled over to the car and that warm glow surrounded us, the glow that always comes and hugs you tight when you have gone out of your way to do the right thing. I bleeped the lock and opened the car door for Aileen, then strolled around to my side with a self-satisfied smirk squirming its sickly way across my face.

A woman knocked on Aileen's window and Aileen pressed the little button that brings it down.

'There you are, love. Glad I caught you.'

She pushed a serviette through the gap and Aileen took it.

'Thank you.'

I started the engine and let off the handbrake and then tried to figure a way out of the car park. Aileen unwrapped the serviette.

'She's given me a sausage roll.'

'Has she?'

Aileen stared hard at her lap.

'Why would she give me a sausage roll?'

'I think she thought we still had the kitten.'

Aileen thought about that for a while.

'He wouldn't have eaten a sausage roll, would he?'

'One woman offered him an egg and cress sand-wich.'

'Did you take it?'

'No.'

'Pity – I like egg and cress.'

She examined the sausage roll closely and then took a tentative bite.

'It was nice of her, wasn't it?'

'Very nice.'

She settled back in her seat and took a much bigger bite.

'How far is it to London?'

'Just over a hundred miles.'

I slipped the car onto the M1 and crossed over to the fast lane. The traffic was getting heavier now and Aileen flinched as the driver of a north-bound lorry slagged off the driver of a Ford Mondeo with a loud blast of his horn.

She polished off the last of the sausage roll and then, after delicately flicking the crumbs from both breasts, settled down for a nice long nap.

S U M M E R

CHAPTER SIX

Aileen was having her nails painted. I had a go at them once, but she said I wasn't supposed to do her knuckles as well and so I haven't been allowed anywhere near them since.

It's one of those jobs, like cutting toenails, that blind people find almost impossible to do. And so Kealen paints them for her now. Kealen is one of those people there ought to be more of. Well there are actually. She is one of eleven. The other ten are Emor, Breithne, Barbara, Bronagh, Dera, Aleran, Nuala, Deirdre, Teffine and Finan.

She's Irish – did I mention that?

I was out in the garden with Thermal, deadheading the roses. Thermal sniffs at them and then I drop them in the bucket – we make a good team. We also listen in to the conversations that float over the hedge from the park.

A woman had been explaining to her husband that the recent spell of good weather was due to all this warmal globing that was going about these days. I had never heard of warmal globing before, but I was going to be sure to keep an eye open for it in future.

They settled down on a bench and she moved on to the subject of home economics.

'You could cut down on the Sunday papers for a start.'

'I couldn't.'

'You could.'

He was very patient with her, but then I suppose he loved her. I can't think of any other possible explanation.

'I only have the *Sunday Times*.'

'Ooh, you little fibber.'

'I'm not.'

'You have dozens of them.'

'It's all the one paper.'

'You must think I'm daft.'

There was a pause while he considered this.

'It has its various sections you see.'

'Mr Lazenby only has the one.'

'He takes the *Sunday Sport*.'

'Well, there you are then.'

I love listening in and if you are very patient and garden very quietly it's a wonderful way to spend an hour or so. Although sometimes it can be rather frustrating.

'You're still with him then?'

'I don't know why – he's only good for one thing.'

'What's that?'

'Countersinking screws. Once I've mastered that – he's off.'

I wanted to rush out of the front gate and chase after the two women. Why on earth would she need a man around, on permanent call, just to countersink screws? Most of us countersink no more than half a dozen screws during the whole of our lifetime. Were they laying new floors throughout the house? Built-in wardrobes perhaps? What on earth could she be on about?

Gradually I have learned to live with the disappointment of not knowing, but it hasn't been easy.

I take comfort in those gems that come sailing over the hedge already topped and tailed, with a beginning, some sort of a middle and a most wonderful end. Like the elderly couple sitting on the bench, sharing an ice-cream cornet.

'Do you want to be buried, or do you want to be cremated?'

'I'm not really bothered, love – surprise me.'

One of the nicest things about going away for a spell is coming home again. I love London and I had thoroughly enjoyed the weekend, but it was good to be back.

We had called in at the Savoy Hotel, the Groucho Club and a posh party in Knightsbridge where we had met lots of old friends who, most of the time, we only ever get to see when they are on television. We wave to them, but they never wave back. I couldn't do that – it's not in my nature.

I had hoped to see Dame Thora Hird. I was working on a play she and I had talked about for some time. But I was out of luck.

'She's away filming. Another series of *Last of the Summer Wine*. She's up in Huddersfield for the next two weeks.'

It's a small world, isn't it? I would give her a chance to settle in and then get in touch with her. In the meantime there were so many important things to be done.

'Thermal, I'm off to buy a lottery ticket – do you want to come with me?'

He was up to his neck in work. He had finished sniffing at the roses, but he still had all the pointing on the steps to examine. At least once a day he spends the best part of half an hour sticking his paw in the holes where it's coming away; he's very thorough. He keeps me abreast of the situation and I appreciate it, even though Aileen says if it wasn't for Thermal the pointing wouldn't be coming away in the first place.

I think he was glad of a break. He nipped off to smarten himself up, sitting high on the stone gatepost, ready for a quick getaway.

'What about you, Arthur? Are you coming?'

Arthur wasn't looking too well. For once he had left his wire brush to fend for itself and he had taken refuge in the lavender bed. He smelled wonderful but his eyes were dull and listless and he looked very old and very tired.

'What's the matter, Arthur?'

I stroked him and he purred, but it was more out of habit than anything else. He must be getting on for sixteen now. He was a pitiful old soul when he hobbled into our lives about four years ago, but those years had fallen away as he grew stronger and more confident. He learned to relax, safe in the knowledge that no-one was going to harm him, and he developed as much of a swagger as those horseshoe-shaped back legs of his were ever going to permit, and now he was quite outgoing, as long as he didn't have to go anywhere.

He never set foot out of the courtyard on his own. Like those holiday-makers abroad who never stray further than the hotel swimming pool, he had spent the last four years within these high stone walls.

The only exception to this rule was if Thermal and I took him over to the edge of the park or up to the garage for a packet of cigarettes or a lottery ticket.

It was always a great adventure. First we had to cross the unadopted road that runs up by the side of the house and then Thermal would dash into Liz's front garden with Arthur hard on his heels.

While I walked along the pavement the pair of them would crash through a series of front gardens, under fences and over hedges, getting well in front of me and then doubling back.

Every now and then Thermal would appear on the top of a wall, right by my shoulder, and I had to pretend to be frightened of him and then he'd run off and do it again a bit further on.

It was great fun and a great day when Arthur got the hang of the idea. He dashed out of a blind driveway, spooked me and then dashed back in again. It was the first time he had ever played in his life and he developed quite a taste for it.

I always crossed the main road to the garage on my own and they would wait for me in the end garden, ready to jump out at me when I passed on my way back. Arthur invariably screwed it up. He would jump out while I was still over on the other side of the road and Thermal would be furious with him.

'You've spoilt it now!'

But Arthur enjoyed himself tremendously, so what the hell. He never played at any other time. We could never tempt him with a table-tennis ball or a toy mouse. Playing equalled running out of a driveway and then running back in again and that was that.

But not today. Maybe he was just tired. I would have a look at him again when I came back.

Kealen took Arthur's place on the walk up to the garage. Thermal wasn't all that impressed – she wasn't half as much fun. For a start she didn't run through the front gardens with him, she walked with me instead and he began to get jealous and do silly things.

He streaked across the road to the park and then streaked straight back again when he saw Mrs Bramley and Nellie out for their afternoon stroll.

Nellie has only recently taken over the job as Mrs Bramley's official canine companion. Poor old Alfred, who had held the post for more years than he cared to remember, had carried on heroically until the very day he died. It's a rotten job looking after Mrs Bramley but somebody has to do it.

Alfred was a grand old chap with the patience of Job, but Nellie still has a lot to learn and she had fallen some way behind, fastened to the end of one of those extending leads that are so popular nowadays.

She was facing the wrong way round and flat on her back with all four of her legs stuck up in the air, which was very brave of her since Mrs Bramley had just come down a flight of stone steps.

Whatever her protest it was completely lost on her owner, who dragged her for yet another ten yards as she came over to have a word with us. We had to look away as Nellie bumped over the pavement edge and then came to a halt in the middle of the road.

I smiled at the little upside-down dog and passed the time of day with her. She had a go at one of those threatening barks she's been practising such a lot lately, but her heart wasn't really in it, so she settled for baring her teeth and left it at that.

'Take no notice,' said Mrs Bramley. 'She's got it on her this morning.'

Kealen and I parted company at the garage. She kissed me on the cheek and then went off on her elegant way, in her black leather jacket and thigh-high boots. I tucked myself onto the end of a short queue waiting by the cash desk, well aware that the others had witnessed her display of affection, and I thought how good it was for my image.

Then I caught a glimpse of my reflection in the window and realized that they must all be thinking what a beautiful granddaughter I had. I bought a newspaper, two scratchcards and a lottery ticket and turned for home.

Thermal planned to mug me the moment I came up alongside the park. I could tell because I had to come up behind him and I could see his little bum wiggling from this side of the hedge long before I reached the corner.

I didn't let on and so he really enjoyed frightening the life out of me. He walked beside me, on top of the wall.

'Has she gone home now?'

'Yes.'

'Better with just the two of us, isn't it?'

I won a pound on the scratchcard and punched the air in triumph. Ridiculous isn't it? They give us our money back and we pretend we've won. Tomorrow I would exchange it for another card and lose. They could give away a million pounds a day and never risk a penny.

I am stuck with the lottery. I gambled on the same set of numbers for the first three weeks and so if I ever missed a week I would know whether I would have won or not. However much of a long shot, I couldn't live with the thought of losing eight and a half million pounds.

My mother would have loved the lottery. She had a flutter every Saturday on the football pools and then she would ring me first thing Sunday morning.

'Deric – I've won the jackpot. I've got thirty-five and a half points.'

Here we go again.

'Mum – you can't have.'

'No honestly. This time I really have. If Everton hadn't scored in the last minute I would have had thirty-six.'

To make life easier for her I had fixed her up with a system – perm any eight from sixteen.

'There was a man last week', she said, 'who won five hundred and twenty-five thousand pounds and he only had twenty-four points.'

Once again I would explain that you didn't count all of the sixteen matches, just the eight results with the highest points. And she would listen, politely. You could almost hear her nodding over the phone as she took it in.

'So you see, Mum – the maximum number of points you can possibly have is twenty-four. You can't get any more than that.'

'I have.'

So I would go over it again and eventually we would reach a compromise. After all I was her son and she didn't want to hurt my feelings.

'I think I can see what you're getting at, but let's wait and see what Littlewoods Pools have to say about it, shall we?'

I made a pot of coffee and then went looking for Aileen. She was sitting by the bed of lavender, stroking Arthur.

'He's not very well, is he?'

'No. If he isn't any better in the morning I'll take him to see the vet.'

And I wasn't looking forward to it. He had only been up to the surgery a couple of times before, but on both occasions he had been absolutely terrified. Whenever I took Thermal to see the vet he quite enjoyed himself. He would stroll around the waiting-room and introduce himself to the other animals.

'I always come here – they're very good, aren't they?'

The other two would be wary and ill at ease, but Arthur simply panicked. He shook all the way there in the car and then sat shivering on my knee in the waiting-room, burying his head under my arm, con-vinced that he would never leave this place alive. By the time I lifted him up onto the table he would be so nervous he could barely stand and once the vet thought he was paralysed.

'Is it his legs?'

'No. He's got a sore mouth.'

I knew nothing of Arthur's past except that he had been badly ill-treated and that when he arrived on our doorstep it had taken us six months to persuade him to come into the house.

'Tell you what, Aileen. I'll ask the vet to come here in the morning.'

As the evening grew chilly, Arthur was still flat out

in the lavender bed and I had to persuade him to come inside. Persuade him as in pick him up and carry him in. He wasn't hungry, he couldn't eat a thing, he said. So I slipped him a secret saucerful of small Icelandic prawns, at which point he admitted to being slightly peckish. He forced them down and promised not to tell the others. I switched on the hall radiator for him and he promised not to mention that either.

He didn't seem to have moved a muscle when I padded in to have a look at him the next morning. I watched carefully for a moment or so to see if he was breathing or not and was pleased to see that the fur on his underbelly was lifting and separating, even though his lungs appeared to be working to rule.

Over breakfast I read a couple of book reviews from the *Daily Telegraph* aloud to Aileen. One gave an author we didn't like very much a right going over and we enjoyed that immensely and then I heard a noise coming from the hall.

I popped out to check up on Arthur once more and found Tigger sitting by his side. She looked like one of those well-bred young ladies who went in for nursing during the First World War – she should have been wearing a starched apron and had an upside-down watch pinned to her chest. When Frink came charging into the hall and wanted to play she had her turned round and back up the stairs almost before she arrived. She made an exception in my case and allowed me to examine the patient.

'*Just two minutes – he needs his rest.*'

Arthur struggled wearily to his feet. He didn't seem to be in pain – just so desperately tired.

'*Right – that's enough. Now let's have you back in bed, young man.*'

He didn't argue. He flopped down onto the carpet, with his back pressed up hard against the radiator. His eyelids came down slowly, one at a time, as though they hadn't spent enough time in rehearsal. Tigger dismissed me with one of her looks.

'We'll be all right. I'll call you if I need you.'

The vet was nowhere near as formidable. Mrs Roger gave the appearance of having all the time in the world and, once she had cleared it with Tigger, she knelt down and examined the patient carefully.

'He's getting on, isn't he?'

'We think he's about sixteen.'

'Yes. That won't be far out.'

She pressed his side and Arthur winced.

'He has a lump.'

She moved her hands all over him and Arthur thought that was extremely pleasant. He purred and was rather disappointed when she stopped. She was in no doubt about what was wrong with him.

'It's a tumour, I'm afraid. He has leukaemia.'

'Oh dear,' I said.

Don't we say some stupid things? Tears immediately sprang to Aileen's eyes and I took a deep breath and tried hard not to follow suit. I am a man and that is what we are supposed to do. It didn't work.

Poor old Arthur. At the hands of humans he had suffered two broken back legs and a broken tail and some twisted idiot once threw a bucket of creosote all over him. And he had coped with all this and still managed to retain his natural dignity and his gentle disposition. Now he had leukaemia and I had said 'oh dear'.

'Is he in pain?' Aileen wanted to know.

'I don't think so. He's just very tired.'

And then, of course, the question Mrs Roger must hear every day of her working life.

'What should we do for the best? Do you think it would be kinder to have him . . .?'

'That's up to you.'

'How long do you think he's got?'

'Don't know. Could be a week – could be months.'

'Is there anything you can do for him?'

She ran her hands over him once more.

'We could try steroids and perhaps a multi-vitamin injection. It might give him a little longer.'

So every day for the next seven days Mrs Roger arrived first thing in the morning and gave Arthur his injections and I think he was rather disappointed when the week finally ground to a halt and there were no further knocks on the front door.

He had taken refuge in Aileen's office, stretched out in front of her gas fire where his meals were brought to him and a saucer of milk was always on tap, just by the brass trivet on the hearth.

First thing every morning I would pop in to have a word with him, anxious to see how, or if, he had struggled through the night, and to bring him his early morning saucer of milk.

On the Sunday morning I pushed open the door a little later than usual, only to find the hearthrug unoccupied and his bedtime milk still untouched and slightly wrinkled – you get the cream off the top of the bottle when you have leukaemia.

My mother once told me that when cats die, they prefer to die in private. They don't want a lot of fuss, she said, so it was with a sinking heart that I began to search under the desk and round the back of the settee.

He came at me like a train from behind the filing cabinet. My sinking heart shot straight into reverse and I nearly died on the spot. He jumped on my foot and then pranced round my legs before making a dash for the open door and the stairs.

From down in the kitchen there came a cry of alarm as a woman in a flimsy nightdress was buzzed by an ancient black cat. She was still wondering what the hell had happened when I arrived on the scene.

'I think Thermal's having one of his daft spells.'

'It wasn't Thermal, love.'

I pushed open the back door and there was Arthur, rolling first on his back and then on his side, playfully chatting up a neglected and rather sullen wire brush.

'Have you missed me? Go on – say you've missed me. My God but you're beautiful.'

I closed the door and picked up the notepad. I would ring Mrs Roger first thing in the morning. I have never liked having needles stuck in my bum, but I had just seen the possibilities and it seemed a small enough price to pay.

CHAPTER SEVEN

Arthur was reborn. It might only be for a short time, but at least the steroid shots and the multi-vitamin injections had given him a new lease of life and he was enjoying every minute of it.

After the first couple of days he slowed down somewhat. He had to – his chassis would never have taken the strain. He strolled about the place, beaming from ear to ear, exchanging pleasantries with the other members of his feline team, even going so far as to allow Chico Mendes O'Connell to have a really good sniff at his wire brush.

It was the best summer we had seen in years and Arthur was determined to live life to the full. He spent each day following the sun around the courtyard until, by early evening, he had hemmed himself into the far corner, sitting as tall as he could possibly manage, taking the last of the fading rays full in the face.

At night I spoilt him as best I could. A month or so before I had found him tucked up on my bed, fast asleep on my pillow, and I didn't really fancy it after that. It isn't a particularly pleasant place to come across a dozing cat, especially one with a marked tendency to dribble in his dreams.

So I had told Aileen that he had dribbled on her pillow and offered to do a swop with her. I would have hers; she could have mine. She thought I was absolutely wonderful and so we exchanged pillows. I felt a bit guilty about it at the time, but then a little guilt never hurt anyone.

But now I stuffed her pillow under his radiator in the hall and bought her a very expensive replacement from Schofields in Leeds and they both thought I was absolutely wonderful. In this life you have to take your opportunities wherever you find them.

The moment Arthur knocked off in the courtyard he would make straight for his newly found feather-filled heaven. He could stretch straight out and still not hang off the far end. He loved it, and the other cats looked on enviously as they passed through the hall every evening on their way home from work.

The story has a downside. From that moment on I was forever running up and down stairs, plucking comatose cats from plumped-up pillows in every bedroom in the house.

'Can't think why we never thought of this before.'

But never mind. Arthur was happy and it might not be for much longer. I hope somebody will do the same for me one day.

I had been hard at work on the play I was trying to write since seven o'clock in the morning and had very little to show for it. Writing is like waiting for a bus – I sit at my desk for hours on end and then, all of a sudden, three sentences come along all at once. I needed a break, so I lit a cigarette and walked over to the window. A thick white mist hung over Greenhead Park, clinging to the ground like a five-foot blanket of virgin snow. It was as though a sight-screen had been hung between the trees.

Above that the sky was of the brightest blue and the sun shone brilliantly, adding a top coat of silver as a finishing touch. August and December teaming up as a double act.

I pushed up the window and looked down onto the garden two storeys below. I could have jumped out and landed safely on the huge white duvet that floated above the stone pavers. I didn't – but I could have.

Over in the park a small pork pie hat took its morning constitutional, floating by without any visible means of support.

As it passed the bandstand it nodded briefly to a head and shoulders walking in the opposite direction. A dog barked frantically – goodness knows what he made of it down there. It was like watching a surreal movie in the making.

Aileen sidled up unheard and put her arm around my shoulder.

'This is fantastic,' I told her. 'I can't even see the hedge this morning.'

She walked over to the desk and began to search for my ashtray, combing the most likely spots with her fingertips.

'Join the club,' she said.

* * *

Arthur was fast asleep when the doorbell rang. He should have been on duty out in the courtyard by now, but he had taken one look at the mist swirling around the rockery and decided to take it in stages this morning.

A young man, old before his time, presented himself on the front doorstep. He wore an anorak at least three sizes too large for him and as he stood there face to face with me, his anorak had already turned to go. The two pieces of string that marked the end of a row of covered buttons were flapping around on the man's left hip, while the vacant hood sat up straight on his right shoulder and whispered desperately into the nearest ear. *'Come on. Let's get out of here. It's not worth it.'*

I smiled and said good morning but the young man hadn't prepared himself to deal with such pleasantries. He had been far too busy marshalling his arguments and my good-natured approach threw him completely. So I smiled at the anorak instead and it blushed and turned away in embarrassment.

The young man pulled himself together, or at least I presume he did. I couldn't see enough of him to be absolutely sure.

'I've got a dog.'

'Have you?'

'Yes.'

'Congratulations.'

I couldn't see a dog anywhere. Perhaps he had it concealed about his person. Such a person could have concealed any number of dogs about his person.

'It's only a little dog.'

'Well – size isn't important, is it?'

'And I come past your house every morning with it.'

73

'Do you?'

'Yes.'

'I see.'

As conversations go this one wasn't going anywhere. I wished he would get on with it. The anorak gave a deep sigh.

'Come on. Get on with it.'

I liked this anorak. It was my kind of anorak.

'You've got a cat, haven't you?'

'Yes. I have four of them.'

'You've got a white one.'

'I have two of those.'

The smaller cat of the two chose that very moment to leap out of the mist and belt along the wall behind him, in blind pursuit of Chico Mendes O'Connell. The anorak noticed, but the man didn't. He pulled himself up to his full height, yet another movement the anorak was able to accommodate without fear of twisting anything.

'Well it's terrorizing my dog.'

His complaint was that at roughly half-past five every afternoon, give or take a few minutes here and there, he would pass by the front of our house accompanied by his faithful little dog Lappie – the name apparently being short for Lapsang Souchong.

As they drew closer the dog would begin to panic because it knew that at any moment now it was going to be jumped on by a ferocious white cat. They never knew where the attacker might be coming from next. One day he would hurl himself from the top of the wall and the following day he would zip out from underneath the hedge or the side gate.

'Couldn't you pick the dog up and carry it, just for a few yards?'

He shook with indignation inside his anorak. The anorak never moved a muscle.

'Why should I?'

'Or cross over to the other side of the road?'

This time his indignation was such that even the anorak suffered from a bout of secondary shaking.

'Why should I?'

Maybe I was wrong, but I tried to explain that this was the real world in which we were living. I couldn't guarantee to have Thermal locked away at half-past five every evening.

'I'm not always around.'

We parted perhaps not the best of friends. He told me that if my cat ever did it again he would shoot it on sight and I told him exactly where I would stick his gun if he even so much as thought about it. To its credit the anorak remained neutral throughout this bitter exchange and as the two of them shuffled off down the path it turned and gave me a broad wink. Or perhaps that was just my imagination.

I wanted to go and have a closer look at the park. Even from down here the mist looked as though you could slice it with a knife. As I walked down the garden steps my legs seemed to disappear from underneath me and by the time I had reached the pavement the mist had reached my waist.

It wasn't quite as deep as I had thought it was going to be – the man in the pork pie hat, the one I had seen from my window, must have been about three feet tall.

On the road itself the passing traffic had cut the mist to ribbons and broken its spirit. It seemed to have little heart for the job. It swirled around in fancy plumes, but it wasn't fooling anyone.

It was only when I stepped over the low wall and into the park that I realized the mist had only been playing at it over on our side.

A policeman's helmet cut its way through the trees and floated across my bow.

A yellow sou'wester detached itself from the trunk of an elderly horse chestnut tree and stepped out to intercept it.

Several cars had pulled up by the kerb, the drivers having climbed out to witness the phenomenon. This was a bonus.

The sou'wester bobbed about on top of the mist in some agitation. Disembodied voices came from underneath the blanket.

'They pinched my brush.'

'Who did?'

'They did.'

'Who's they?'

'Them as pinched my brush.'

From that point on the conversation continued in fits and starts.

'I only realized it had gone when they held it up and started waving it at me from over there.'

'What sort of brush was it?'

'My yard brush – I was sweeping up the leaves.'

The drivers glanced at one another and then down at their feet, trying to imagine a man sweeping up leaves on a morning like this. A pause told us that the policeman was obviously playing with the same image.

'Where was your brush at the time?'

'Propped up by the side of my cart.'

'And whereabouts was your cart?'

The sou'wester then turned through a full 360 degrees in an attempt to establish its bearings. It was the most amazing thing we had witnessed so far. I once saw a ventriloquist's dummy do it on the television, but this was a first as far as a human being was concerned. We almost gave him a round of applause.

'They could have pinched that as well.'

The two of them disappeared out of earshot to see if they could find the cart, and one by one the drivers broke up and climbed back into their cars.

They should have stayed on. The pork pie hat suddenly appeared out of the mist and made its way up the slope towards me. A tight-fitting hacking jacket followed closely on its heels and then a pair of cavalry twill trousers pounded up the incline.

The man had a pipe clamped firmly between his teeth – he could have been Jacques Tati playing Monsieur Hulot if you made a few allowances. He passed the time of day with me.

'Na then.'

Well, a Yorkshire Monsieur Hulot anyway. A passer-by recognized him.

'Hey up, Wilf.'

'Hey up, Reg.'

That clinched it. Monsieur Wilf Hulot.

As he climbed over the wall he switched something from hand to hand. An extending dog lead, just like the one Mrs Bramley uses when she takes Nellie out for her morning drag. It stretched way back into the mist and so far there seemed to be nothing attached to the other end.

Then a tail cut through the surface like the radio mast on a submarine. It circled the steep embankment once or twice and then disappeared from view. Wilf yanked on the lead and shouted into the void.

'Come on, you daft bat.'

Nothing happened. The man turned to me.

'He does it to be awkward, you know. Sits down when he's had enough.'

He yanked again.

'I have to be careful. He can work his collar off if he's half a mind to. Puts his chin up and flattens his ears.'

This time he gave just the gentlest of tugs, but even so it was a tug too far. The lead went slack and when he pressed the button it wound in on itself – the empty collar hanging like a noose from his hands.

'Oh, bloody hell.'

He dived back into the mist with the resigned air of a soldier going over the top.

'Just you wait until I get my hands on you. I'll kill you. Come on now – there's a good boy.'

I turned to go home.

'Don't think I can't see you. Where are you, you daft devil?'

He was still at it as I crossed back over the road.

'I'll kill you. I will. I'll kill you.'

I closed the garden gate behind me.

'Come on, you stupid sod – there's a good boy.'

A few moments later I was back in my office on the second floor, looking out over the park once more.

A battered old mongrel staggered out of the mist, had a good long cough to clear his tubes and then shook himself with remarkable vigour for a dog of his age. He plonked his bottom down on the low wall and gazed in silent wonder as the pork pie hat foraged about in the mist.

'Come on, Rover – where the hell are you?'

By late morning the mist had cleared and within minutes there appeared a whole flotilla of small dogs, being ushered in all directions by elderly ladies in sensible shoes and elderly gentlemen in anything but a rush.

It's always the same. The mornings belong to the grey brigade, those who have retired from the work-a-day world and who seem to specialize in canines of the vertically challenged variety.

In the early evening it is the taller and more elegant dogs of this world that are in evidence. Golden retrievers and well-bred Alsatians are decanted from the claustrophobic warmth of the estate car, out onto the cool green acres of the park, there to pose and prance like eager teenagers out on the razzle.

But at eleven-thirty in the morning it's the stately parade of the short-arsed brigade that catches the eye. Chunky-thighed Sealyhams and short portly corgis take a slow and dignified turn around the playing area, rarely straying from the path except to crouch on the neatly trimmed grass every now and then, leaving behind them the sort of trophy that would bring tears to the eyes of an adult buffalo.

I made a pot of tea and took the tray into Aileen's office. She was talking on the phone, but as I pushed open the door she broke off guiltily, cupping her hand over the mouthpiece. Probably one of her many lovers – better leave her to it.

She whispered through her fingers. 'Do you mind hanging on for a moment?'

And then she turned to me and smiled the most beautiful smile and I thanked my lucky stars that I had managed to grab her before any of the others had a chance.

'I want to buy you a surprise for our anniversary,' she said, 'but I need to know something first.'

She has trouble arranging surprises – with the colour of things or whether they will fit into this space or that.

'Promise me you won't ask any supplementary questions or you'll guess what it is.'

'I promise.'

She paused for a moment, arranging the words in her head so that they wouldn't give anything away.

'If we had a satellite dish – where would you put it on our roof?'

I suggested the balcony outside the third-floor bedroom window.

'Then you wouldn't see it from the road.'

She thought that was a very good idea and I refrained from asking any supplementary questions. I like surprises and wondered what on earth my anniversary present could possibly be.

Thermal and I spent the rest of the afternoon together. He sat on my desk for a while, watching the words as they popped up onto the screen. He likes words and he tries to catch them.

'Move over a bit – I can't see what I'm doing.'

He likes catching words but he pretends he has no idea what they mean, especially when those words have been strung together into a popular phrase or saying, such as – 'get off that chair with your filthy paws. Have you any idea what that settee cost?' Or, 'move over a bit – I can't see what I'm doing' – so I picked him up and sat him down to one side, under the desk lamp.

He busied himself for a while with a useful elastic band that I had fastened around the base of the lamp. It's a yellow one, about a foot long and it's going to come in very handy one of these days.

'Come here – you'll break it.'

I stretched him out on my knee and he would have been perfectly comfortable as he was, but no, he had to go and turn around three times before settling down, each time flirting his ear against the ornate key that sticks out from the desk drawer.

'Are you finished?'

He purred and dug his claws into that little roll of fat that has crept out unnoticed just above my left hip. It's nothing to worry about – I can make it disappear whenever I want. I just have to hold my back perfectly straight, stand on one leg and take a deep breath.

Then Thermal gave a heavy sigh and his chin sank deep into my forearm, right up to his eyeballs. I don't know how cats do that. Whenever they lie down their bodies seem quite capable of passing straight through a small shag-pile hearthrug, a thick Axminster carpet and a good two and a half inches of Duralay. And then when you try and pick them up it's as though their bodies have been velcroed to the floorboards.

He purred contentedly and gazed up into my eyes.

'This is nice, isn't it?'

'Very nice.'

I wrapped my left foot over my right foot and squeezed my knees together. His bum was beginning to slide down between my legs, so I brought my heels back until they were tucked in under the base of the chair.

'It's like old times – just the two of us.'

'It is, isn't it.'

He gave my roll of fat a gentle squeeze with his claws.

'We must do this more often.'

And so we should. Once upon a time, when there were just the two of us around and Thermal was but a short stumpy kitten, we had a strict daily routine

81

which involved a thirty-minute workout with a table-tennis ball, a ritual bashing of the pull switch in the bathroom and then on to a session of toilet flushing in which he tried to catch the water as it cascaded down the pan.

His best friend had been a sultana called Ralph and the three of us had some high old times together. We played hide and seek. I would hide Ralph and Thermal would have to seek him – we never played it the other way round, it would have taken for ever.

But now I had three other cats to cope with and, besides, Thermal had long since put his childish ways behind him. He took his career in mouse management very seriously these days and what with all the over-time involved there just weren't enough hours available for playing around.

It was all work with him nowadays, apart from sleeping and eating and jumping off high walls onto very small dogs. I glanced at my watch. It was twenty-five minutes past five.

'Hey. Come on. That dog should be going past any minute.'

We didn't have to wait long. Way down below me I could see an anorak striding along the pavement, an anorak with a dog on a lead, the smallest dog I have ever seen in my life. It was a hairless something or other and it looked just like a rat on castors.

'Thermal, how could you?'

'*What?*'

'Beat up a dog like that – it's pathetic.'

'*I've never seen it before in my life.*'

'Oh come on now.'

He gave me one of his innocent looks, but he wasn't fooling anyone. Good job I had him up here with me, sealed in behind the double glazing. A safe passage this evening might go some way towards defusing the animosity – I can't be doing with arguments.

The anorak had reached the danger zone but the little dog was hanging back, stretching the short lead to breaking point. Or stretching the little dog to breaking point more likely – the animal would have snapped first, being the thinner of the two.

But then nothing happened and the pair of them began to relax. The anorak seemed to lose a pound and a half of pressure and one could sense that there might even be a human being in there – even the lead went slack as the little dog caught up and then trotted ahead.

It was a big mistake. There came the sound of screeching paws and then a small ball of white fur flew around the corner and planted itself across their path.

'It's Frink.'

'Told you it wasn't me.'

'Sorry about that.'

'It's all right.'

With her back arched and her legs as tall as poplar trees the kitten looked like a rather small but extremely lethal viaduct. The dog looked aghast. He had been yanked up out of harm's way and swung in mid air from the end of his lead, round and round, like a conker on a piece of string.

By the time I had nipped down two flights of stairs and out of the front door it was all over and Frink was telling Arthur all about it.

'So I said, make my day, punk.'

'You didn't?'

'I did. I told him. I said this street ain't big enough for both of us.'

'*You didn't?*'
'*I did.*'

I blame the television. *Gladiators* for Frink's new-found aggression and *The Victoria Wood Show* for the dialogue. Tigger was brought up on *All Creatures Great and Small* and the *Antiques Roadshow* and she's turned out to be a proper little lady.

Thermal was reared on *Blue Peter* and he can now turn his paw to almost anything. He can craft a perfectly acceptable scratching post out of a couple of empty cigarette packets and the tube from a toilet roll, whereas Arthur's life has been completely untouched by the wicked media – which is why he remains such an innocent soul at heart and is just about as thick as a bucket.

CHAPTER EIGHT

I sat for a while in Choosies, nursing a cup of coffee, pretending not to listen to the two women at the next table. The one with the white Peter Pan collar poking out from underneath her navy-blue jumper was telling the other one about her trip around the world.

'I knew it was going to be a mistake before we set off.'

Perhaps she should have gone somewhere else. She leaned in to her subject, tapping the table with a small cake fork.

'You can always tell whether a country's civilized or not – just by the state of their grass verges.'

She may have a point there. You only have to watch the nine o'clock news. Some of those grass verges in Bosnia are a damn disgrace. And as for those in Groznyy – well those Chechens ought to be shot.

She hadn't a good word to say about Cairo – apparently there was a lot of sand about and she hadn't been expecting that.

'And when you've seen one pyramid, you've seen them all.'

'Did you go up the Nile?'

'Well, Jack said we did – but it wasn't always easy to tell.'

It took some time to pay the bill. A kid in a pushchair had taken over the ground floor and I couldn't work my way around her. They just don't think, these kids. She was so tiny you could have dropped her in a jam pot and yet with her teddy bear, a comfort blanket and two spare anoraks she occupied half the bloody shop. You would have thought she owned the place. Good job her daddy did. Her mummy smiled at me. She was a very attractive mummy and I decided to let the kid off, this time anyway. I told her parents a very funny story about my granddaughter Katie and then they told me one about a kid they knew:

'Do we have to eat in the dying-room?'

'It's not the dying-room, darling – it's the dining-room.'

'No it's not. It's the dying-room. If this is the living-room, then that must be the dying-room.'

I gave the teddy bear a sharp kick on my way out. It was a much better story than the one I had told. My granddaughter had better get her act together – either shape up or ship out, that's what I say.

As I entered St George's Square I paused for a moment, plonking my bottom down on a seat next to a rather ancient bag lady. On second thoughts maybe she wasn't a bag lady at all. There was no doubting the fact that she had a bag with her – I was sitting on it. The 'lady' however was less in evidence.

'You're sitting on my effin' bag.'

'Sorry.'

'I should effin' well think so.'

She rummaged through her belongings to see if they were still in one piece and I sat and cast an appreciative eye over Huddersfield's magnificent railway station. John Betjeman thought it was the most wonderful building and it is – as long as you don't go inside. It's as though someone presented the town with a box of Thornton's Continental and then went and stuffed it full of Maltesers.

My newly found friend removed a couple of plastic trays from her bag, each containing half a dozen Marks and Spencer tandoori chicken drumsticks. You must have seen them. In the Huddersfield branch of Marks and Spencer they are stacked just by the door leading out into King Street. It's very convenient for those who believe that tills are nothing but a waste of time. A pigeon came over to investigate.

'Eff off,' she told him.

And so he effed off towards the railway station and I effed off with him. He flew and I walked, but I got there first because apparently straight lines have no place whatsoever in a pigeon's culture.

I found another bench and the pigeon found me. I found a half-empty packet of cheese and onion crisps in the litter-bin by my elbow and dropped a couple under the bench for him. The pigeon had found a friend for life, or three minutes – whichever was the longer.

You can't travel straight to London by rail from
Huddersfield. The line runs east to west, so you have
to change at Wakefield Westgate. I didn't know that
when I first moved here.

'What time's the next train to Halifax?'

'I've no idea, lad – last one were over forty years ago.'

I usually drive over to Wakefield and leave the car
there – anything to avoid being stuck for an unpleasant half an hour or so on one of those two-carriage
sprinter trains with their orange stripes and their hard
seats and that 'stuff you mate, you're only a passenger' feel that they have about them.

As Bill Bryson wrote in *Notes From a Small Island*,
'Why would anyone think that train passengers
would like to be surrounded by a lot of orange, particularly first thing in the morning?'

But today my car was in intensive care down at
Rocar Moores and so here I was, surrounded not only
by a sunburst of day-glo orange but also by a young
man who had his shirt-tail hanging out over quilted
black trousers that concertina'd all the way down
from his crutch to his ankles.

It's the fashion at the moment, especially with
young blacks, to buy a pair of trousers for a man of six
feet eight inches and then wear them yourself. I heard
an old-age pensioner say to her husband, only a
couple of days ago, 'Whoever measured his inside leg
ought to be shot. Do you think I should tell him?'

'I wouldn't, love – not if I were you.'

Have you ever noticed that it is quite possible to be
surrounded by a single human being. This one, along
with his trousers, had me cornered up against the cold
mid-morning glass. He was huge. No matter where I

looked there was a part of him, hemming me in, taking my space, threatening me in such a way, with both his body language and his body odour, that I wondered whether my heart or my nostrils would be the first to give in.

I made contingency plans in case I was about to be mugged. I would hide in his trousers until he got off at Wakefield and then make a break for it.

'Can you split me a ten-pound note for two fivers?'

Here we go. I wasn't getting my wallet out for anything. It was staying where it was, butted up to my pounding heart. Mind you – there were just the two of us in the whole carriage and he was big enough to take it if he wanted to.

'Sorry. I've only got tens and twenties.'

What on earth made me say that? What a stupid thing to say. Serve me right now if he turned me inside out.

'They'll be able to change it for you at Wakefield.'

'I shan't have time.'

There followed a silence that could have had menace written all over it – but somehow it didn't. I watched his face and it was working something or other over, but I knew for certain it wasn't me.

'What's the problem?'

'It's the taxi.'

'There'll be plenty at Wakefield.'

'I know. I get one every week or so – to a bridge over the M1 where a coach picks me up. It costs round about three pound fifty and I wanted a fiver for the driver.'

'He'll be able to change you a tenner.'

The train, for want of a better word, pulled into one of those small scruffy stations that are scattered like commas along the branch lines of West Yorkshire. You get the feeling that the last thing it expected to see this morning was a train, and if only it had known one was coming it would have tarted itself up a bit. No-one got on and no-one got off and my travelling companion moved in a little closer as he confided his innermost secrets.

'You see I'm hopeless at it.'

'What?'

'Tipping. If I give him a fiver and it comes to three pounds seventy-five, then I can walk away and let him keep the rest.'

'Well if you give him a tenner, keep the fiver and give him the loose change.'

'I can't. I've tried it. I stand there watching him going through his pockets, trying to find the right money, and I get all embarrassed and then I hear a voice telling him to keep the change – and then I realize it's me talking.'

'That's almost twice as much again as the fare.'

'I know. It's the same in hotels. I can't go in lifts. A man once said, "What floor do you want?" and I told him and he pressed a button and I gave him a tip. He didn't want to take it, but I made him and afterwards I realized he was just staying there like me. I hardly came out of my room after that.'

He didn't look at all threatening now. The body odour would still have melted lead at forty paces, but I could forgive him that. He looked up.

'My mum and dad never went anywhere where you had to tip anyone. On the buses and down the Legion and that was about the size of it.'

I put my hand in my pocket. I had five one-pound coins in there – in case I had to tip anyone.

'Here you are. Use that.'

'I can't just . . .'

'Doesn't matter.'

He took my name and address and promised to post it on to me. Then he gave me his name – care of one of the most prestigious rugby league clubs in the land. I had heard of him. I had seen him on the television, covered in mud. He's very well known. He thanked me profusely and said that he had never heard of me.

I'll say this for those gaudy little sprinters, you don't half appreciate the comfort of the InterCity 125 afterwards. I spread myself out, tried to make myself as big as the man in the trousers and it worked. I had a whole table to myself, and once the train had pulled out of Wakefield station and the danger of any further boarders had safely passed, I wobbled off down the aisle to ring Aileen.

The yuppy image of mobile phones has been well and truly earned over the past few years, but now that fourteen-year-old schoolboys are using them to call one another from right over on the other side of the classroom, let's hope it won't be long before they are downgraded in status, to say that of the biro. Or better still, the cotton-wool bud – something you wouldn't want to pull out in public.

On my last trip down to London there was a young estate agent sitting a couple of rows in front of me. In striped shirtsleeves and a very loud voice he rang just about everyone else in the country – I dreaded the thought that he might get round to me eventually.

The rest of us muttered under our breath, raised our eyebrows to one another across the aisle, sighed deeply and even glared at him as we passed on our way down for coffee and back.

On and on he went, until eventually a sweet old

man with a walking-stick hauled himself to his feet and, wobbling from side to side as the train thrashed its way through the Nottinghamshire countryside, made his way down the carriage towards the young man.

A fat forefinger was just about to push another set of selected buttons when the walking-stick came down hard on the table.

'Use that thing once more, young man, and it goes straight up your arse.'

There were no more calls after that and we tried to catch the old man's eye as he stumbled back to his seat, to show our approval, but he was having none of it. We had let a frail old soul fight our battle for us and he was not impressed. Neither were we. We were thoroughly ashamed of ourselves.

But I must say I wouldn't be without mine for the world. With a blind wife it has become an absolute must. She can ring me in emergencies:

'I can't find my cigarettes.'

'They were on top of the bread bin right after breakfast.'

And with just one call I can make life that much easier for her, which is why I was making my way down the aisle. I always ring from that bit in between the carriages, where the toilet doors swing loosely in the breeze and the suitcases slide softly to and fro, along the luggage racks.

I had six sheets of A4 paper with me and I shuffled through them as I dialled the number. Aileen has a cordless phone and it never leaves her side.

'Hello.'

'Hello, love. Ready for lunch?'

'Give me just a minute.'

We chatted as she made her way downstairs from her study, down towards the kitchen.

'Nick rang.'

'Nothing wrong, is there?'

'No. He was just checking.'

I still panic whenever the kids ring up. It's a throw-back from the old days.

'I'm in Chesterfield Royal Hospital, Dad, but you're not to worry. The motorbike swerved just in time – it was only the side-car that hit me.'

Sally was just as bad, with her reverse-charge calls from over on the other side of the world.

'Whatever you hear on the news, Dad, don't you believe it – it was only a very small earthquake.'

Aileen told me that she was now in position, so phase one of our finely tuned operation swung smoothly into action.

'What do you fancy?'

'I think the chicken tikka masala sounds rather nice.'

'Right.'

I shuffled through my sheets of paper until I found the one I wanted.

'Top shelf, left-hand side, bottom packet.'

I heard the milk bottles rattle as the fridge door swung open.

'Oops!'

'What's wrong?'

'Celery.'

'It always does that.'

'Got it.'

'Right.'

I turned my attention back to the sheet of paper. If I am going to be away for the night I stack the fridge with microwaveable dishes, making a note of the position of each one. Then I photocopy the packet sleeves, back and front, so that I have all the instructions to hand.

'I shall need some rice with it.'

'OK.'

'Saffron I think.'

I found the saffron sheet. On the top it stated 'times two'.

'Middle shelf, in the middle. They are both saffron.'

'Got it.'

'Right.'

The chicken tikka masala looked really good, even in black and white, and my stomach began to waken from a deep sleep. I turned the sheet upside down and began to read the instructions.

'Remove cover and film.'

There was a short pause.

'Just a minute – I'll go and get the video camera.'

I can be a bit slow at times.

'How do you mean?'

'Remove cover and film.'

I got it now and we both laughed. We like a joke, especially if Aileen has made it. She gets so much pleasure out of repeating the stories in private and I love watching her face as she works her way towards the punch-line. Then I repeat the stories in public and get paid for it. It's a pleasant life.

She sounded a bit dubious.

'Usually you have to pierce the film.'

'Not with this one. Remove film and replace loosely, then microwave for four minutes.'

'You're the boss.'

She took the little dish over to the oven. We have dotted the various buttons with a sort of sealing wax from the RNIB and devised a personal Braille system that works rather well. Aileen's fingers have never come to terms with the normal Braille layout, they don't seem to be sensitive enough. Our particular version uses great lumps of the stuff so that it sticks out like the peaks of icing sugar on a child's birthday cake – you could read it with your elbows.

I heard four short pings and then a sudden lurch as the turntable began to revolve. Aren't microwave ovens wonderful things? With the conventional oven Aileen used to burn herself on a regular basis. Now she can produce an excellent Indian or Chinese dish in just four minutes flat and the only danger she faces is that, sometime in the future, the boffins will go and tell us that microwave ovens have been causing cancer in mice for the past ten years.

We dealt with the saffron rice – you had to pierce the film with that one – and then we popped the chicken masala back in for a quick ten seconds.

'May I suggest an amusing little Riesling – it's in the fridge, behind the Buxton water.'

'Yes, I know. I've had a glass and a half already.'

The mobile phone comes in very handy even when we are out together. The last time we were down in London I had to travel over to Ealing to see my publishers. Aileen had a meeting with a producer at the BBC and we had agreed to meet up afterwards in a bookshop – she's invariably late and I thought I could spend the time browsing.

After half an hour she still wasn't there and I began to worry, so I dialled her mobile phone. She answered as soon as she could – she has one hell of a handbag.

'Hello.'

'Hello, love – where are you?'

She paused for a moment and then I heard her ask a passer-by.

'Excuse me. Where exactly am I?'

She came back to me as soon as she had thanked the stranger.

'*Crime and Punishment,*' she said.

I took two paces to my left and peered round the end of the bookshelves and there she was. As I said, I wouldn't be without my mobile phone – I don't know what I would do without it.

CHAPTER NINE

The taxi driver dropped me off just a few blocks short of the Groucho Club in Dean Street. He could have taken me right up to the front door, but I like that little walk through Chinatown. Daylight only offers a watered-down version of the real thing; the place only comes alive after dark has fallen, but even so it makes one hell of a change after Huddersfield.

I must have read a couple of dozen menus in as many restaurant windows in as many yards before I went head over heels over the cyclist sitting on the pavement.

He wore the full regalia. The bedpan on his head, the knee pads, the elbow pads, and where there was neither plastic nor rubber there was Lycra.

I should think it takes all the fun out of it. I remember when twelve-year-old kids wore nothing but the shortest of shorts, an open-neck shirt and a pair of flapping sandals, their satchels rattling against the flashing spokes as they raced home from school. They wore their bloody knees as a badge of honour, and yet nowadays grown men pedal around in broad daylight looking as though they have just failed the audition for *Gladiators*.

All the same I apologized. I always do. I was born guilty. The cyclist accepted my apology with an air of detachment, as though he wasn't aware that I had just grazed my nose on the pavement beside him.

'That's OK.'

He was staring at an electric-blue bicycle that had been chained to a nearby lamppost. The chain itself was covered in see-through plastic and the lock wouldn't have seemed out of place had it been dangling from the back door of a Securicor van.

'What's wrong?'

'I've lost the key.'

I tried to help. I wondered if we might thread the bike up the lamppost and then ease it off over the top. Apparently he had thought of that and decided it was a non-starter.

'Hacksaw then?'

I was having trouble getting through to him. He just sat there, rattling the chain as though that might help, so I decided to leave him to it. There was a Thai restaurant only a few yards away and I couldn't wait to get at the menu.

'See you.'

The menu was spread out in a display case by the main door. Four pages long it was, and I digested every last morsel, I couldn't have read another thing. When

I turned to go he was still there, squatting on the pavement. It's not every day that you come across a man who has gone and locked himself out of his bicycle.

I like the Groucho Club. It takes a bit of stick every now and then from *Private Eye* magazine. They have it down as a watering-hole for luvvies, but when you come in from out of town, then it's nice to have somewhere where you can sink down into a cosy armchair, read the papers and watch the passing parade of well-known faces.

At the next table sat a publisher, a leading literary agent and a well-known fraudster whose face had been plastered right across the front pages during the past few weeks. He was about to be treated to the best of everything and he was loving every minute of it. We used to boo and hiss the villains and now we buy their books. Sad isn't it?

I picked up the menu. The food's good and quite reasonable as London prices go and mobile phones are not only frowned upon, they are barred completely – and that goes for autograph hunters as well. And they can be a real nuisance. I often have to chase after them for miles, pin them down, and then sit on their faces before they can be persuaded to let me sign their grubby little books.

So it was something of a surprise when I heard a voice behind me enquiring, 'You're him, aren't you?'

Well, perhaps not so surprising. I have been mistaken for Michael Bentine, Bernard Cribbins and even Rolf Harris in my time, but unfortunately never for Robert Redford.

'You are. You're that writer. I've read every one of your books, I think they're wonderful. You're Deric Longden, aren't you?'

'Er yes.'

I turned to receive my due acclaim, smiling, but in a rather modest way you understand.

My son can be a real pain in the neck at times. I ought to have had him thrown out, but I didn't. He came closer.

'Did you know you've grazed your nose?'

'Yes.'

'It suits you.'

I told him to go and claim our table in the dining-room, while I sorted out my mobile phone and a couple of photocopied sheets of A4 paper.

'I'll join you in a minute or so, Nick. I've just got to pop outside and feed Aileen.'

Lunch at the Groucho and then on to a business dinner at Orso's later that evening and still I woke at the crack of dawn, desperate for eggs, bacon, sausage and fried bread.

At home it's a slice of toast and a cup of coffee, but whenever I am away I yearn for a cooked breakfast. It's like a drug. I can see the sausage glistening on my plate as I pull up outside the hotel the evening before, the thick slices of bacon sizzling in between a couple of farm-fresh eggs. I have been known to wipe away a tear when the fried bread turns out to be all soft and bendy and not as crisp as I would have liked it to be.

And so I was already in the dining-room, poised for action, as the waitresses yawned and set about making the first pot of coffee of the morning. In no time at all the young woman in charge of my case brought me a job lot, with extra mushrooms and hash browns, and hoped that I would have a nice day in a Filipino accent.

It was a wonderful day. I jumped on the tube some-where close by and jumped off somewhere a long way away. I like to wander around the far side, down little lanes I have never seen before and will never see again, to come across leafy squares and squalid backstreets, anywhere that takes my fancy. I had at least four hours to kill before going over to Ealing to see my publishers and the sun was shining.

I stopped a man to ask him where I was, but he had no idea. He said he had come over from Trinidad fourteen years ago and was just getting to grips with the place.

'Did you know your nose is bleeding?'

'Yes. I keep dabbing it.'

There was an open market, he told me, just down there and then first right he thought it was, and then turn off left at the pub.

'You'll hear it long before you see it.'

'Thanks.'

There were more pubs than there were houses and more open spaces than there were pubs. It was as though they hadn't bothered since the Blitz. The arches under a railway bridge had been bricked up and turned into makeshift business premises.

Most of them had been closed down, but just along the road a pair of huge double gates swung half open; 'Stone' being written on one of them and 'Mason' on the other. In the interests of marketing someone had taken the trouble to paint in large letters, on a sheet of bare hardboard, the slogan 'Fireplaces – made to measure'.

I poked my head into the yard and saw row upon row of paving-stones leaning up against the wall and wondered if any of them were mine.

Just over a month before, I had woken in the small hours to the noise of a lorry being driven away. I checked the doors and windows and then the court-yard round the back, but nothing untoward seemed to have happened.

Next morning I went to get the car from the garage and then quickly raced back indoors.

'Aileen. We've had burglars. Somebody's stolen the pavement.'

Over fifty square metres of York stone pavers had disappeared, just like that. And it's a private road, so they were our responsibility. The policeman sympathized.

'They'll probably be in London by this time. Worth a fortune down there, they are.'

I took a closer look, wishing that I had carved my initials on each and every one of them. A voice behind me wanted to know if it could be of any assistance.

'Do you sell them?'

'Not if I can help it. They're like gold, you know. Worth more to me if I make fireplaces out of them.'

'How much if you did?'

'Forty-five quid a square metre. You provide the transport.'

'I'll think about it.'

I thought about it all the way down to the market. Forty-five quid, times fifty.

Let me see – that's £2,250. I dabbed a drop of blood off my nose with a sheet of toilet paper I had stolen from the hotel. Hardly a fair exchange, I thought.

I never made it to the market. I stopped to buy a newspaper. Over the years I have discovered that you never find a newsagent's shop anywhere near a café, the two don't seem to go together, so I armed myself with a copy of the *Daily Telegraph*, ready for the golden moment when I found a cup of coffee that hadn't come out of a jar.

What I found instead was a rather disreputable dog. He was sniffing a lamppost when I first laid eyes on him. I think it was the professional way in which he went about his job of sniffing that caught my eye. He looked as though he knew what he was doing – he didn't rush things, didn't try to take the lamppost by surprise. There was an easy confidence about his approach that immediately put the lamppost at its ease. You could tell he was about to sniff when he was still fully five yards away, so there was no danger of that unexpected wet nose that can so easily fluster a lamppost of a nervous disposition.

He was a cross between something and God knows what. Some sort of wire-haired terrier had been consulted at the design stage, but there was no doubt he'd had a lot of help, and nature had decided upon a delicate mix of nicotine-brown with off-white patches. One of those patches had settled around his left eye, which gave him a sort of cock-eyed cockney look that went well with the hustle and bustle of the East End of London.

On impulse I decided to follow him. He obviously took the same route every morning. Shopkeepers setting out their wares passed the time of day with him and street cleaners nodded in his direction as he trotted by. A wino offered him a drink from his bottle but the little dog ignored him and carried on.

If he hadn't stopped to sniff at every single lamppost I wouldn't have been able to keep within shouting distance of him. But after a while he seemed to realize that I had tagged on behind him and he began to sit down and wait for me at street corners.

He didn't make a show of it. He simply exaggerated the time it took for him to look left and right before he crossed over the road. Earlier on he had hardly bothered, a cursory glance without even breaking step had been all that was needed. But now he planted his bottom down on the pavement and studiously examined the flow of traffic from either direction. Then he would glance over his shoulder to see if I was still with him before setting off again.

Soon the streets began to narrow and it was more or less just him and me. Then he disappeared and I backtracked and peered down a passage that I had barely noticed a few moments earlier. He was waiting for me. In fact, he was on his way back up the passage to see where the hell I'd got to.

It was the first time I had managed to get up really close. He was nothing but a bag of bones, held together by loose skin and dignity, not a dog who had been badly treated, just old and well past his sell-by date. I stuck to his tail until we reached the other end of the passage and emerged into a pool of brilliant sunlight and another London altogether.

It was like going back in time. There was a church and what might pass for a village green. A row of tiny white cottages fringed a cobbled square, standing like ornamental teapots in a Stratford antique shop.

The little dog didn't hang about. There wasn't a lamppost in sight and maybe he was suffering withdrawal symptoms. He scurried past the row of cottages and then seemed to disappear through the blank wall of a three-storey house.

I ran after him to find he'd cut off down a tight little alley-way between two of the houses and was now making an emergency stop, with his leg cocked high against a cracked fall pipe.

He barked indignantly, telling me to hurry up.

'*Woof.*'

It isn't easy to explain how indignant he sounded, not even in italics.

The houses stood only a few feet apart from each other and seemed to be making a great effort to hold hands. The alley-way was just a little wider than my shoulders and, halfway along its path, the walls bulged outwards so that I had to shimmy sideways for a yard or two. Iron straps had been bolted to the brickwork in a vain attempt to hold back this middle-aged spread, but they were fighting a losing battle, and a shiver ran up my spine as I picked my way along.

The sky was too narrow and too high to be of any comfort, but the grey light at the end of the alley-way grew larger all the time and soon I found myself standing in a small cemetery that must have been dead for years.

The people who had been buried here didn't want anyone to think they were enjoying themselves. It was overgrown and dank and miserable, although my friend tried to liven things up by peeing on selected headstones. Then he went off through a gap in the hedge and I was only too happy to follow him.

He led me through a maze of quiet streets and sober squares, past ivy-covered walls and window-boxes so packed with blooms they looked as though they might explode at any moment. I could have been in Harrogate. And everyone had a word for the little dog as he bounced along the pavement.

'Morning, Paddy.'

'Hello, boy.'

'You here again, Scruffy?'

'There's a good dog.'

Whatever his name he certainly knew what he was doing, so it came as no surprise when he did a sharp right turn and marched straight in through the front door of a café.

By the time I reached the counter he was being presented with a free sausage roll. At least I assume it was free, I hadn't noticed him carrying any cash about his person. Of course, I could be doing him an injustice – maybe he used his credit card.

He paused on his way out, settled down by my left foot, and then began to eat his sausage roll. The proprietor leaned over his counter.

'Not in here, boy – take it outside.'

The dog took no notice and the proprietor noticed me for the first time.

'He's not yours, is he?'

'No. We're just out for a walk together.'

The dog had a good stretch, leaned himself up against my leg and began to search his fur with his tongue for bits of flaky pastry that had gone missing. He seemed to know just how many bits of flaky pastry the average sausage roll should contain.

'I didn't think he was yours – he comes in here most days. I shouldn't have him in really – I'd be for it if the man from the hygiene put his head round the door.'

The dog nuzzled my fingers and looked up at me, his eyes turning to liquid. I ordered three sausage rolls and a cup of coffee.

'And he doesn't half stink – have you noticed?'

At that moment the dog broke wind. At least the café owner knew him well enough and wouldn't think it was me. Thankfully he didn't seem to notice at all.

'It's not his fault that he smells, mind you. He's a nice little dog. It's just that he's getting on a bit. My mother-in-law's just the same.'

I took the sausage rolls out to a table on the pavement, with a promise that the coffee would follow shortly.

'This 'ere's been standing for a while.'

We ate in silence. I sat at the plastic table and nibbled my sausage roll from a patterned paper plate. The dog sat underneath the table and nibbled the other two from a well-worn paving-stone. For such a scruffy erk he had the most delicate pavement manners.

An old man stopped and stooped to pat him and the dog broke off for a brief moment to appreciate the gesture.

'There you are, old chap – that's for afters.'

The old man didn't offer me a toffee, but then I didn't have to lick the back of his hand. There's always a price to pay.

We sat for a while together, observing the passing scene, and then he gave a big long stretch and nudged himself up against my knee.

He wasn't one for long goodbyes. One minute we were a double act and the next he had melted away, filtering in amongst a forest of legs.

I watched him slip across the road and then drift into the cake shop almost opposite. My coffee arrived and the proprietor kindly wiped my spoon on his apron before placing it on the saucer.

'Doesn't half stink in there – I've had to put the fan on.'

He glanced under the table.

'Has he gone?'

'Yes.'

'I shouldn't encourage him really. Just feel sorry for him. I don't think he gets enough to eat.'

Across the road the dog padded out of the cake shop alongside a rather well-padded lady. He waited patiently while she dug deep into a white paper bag and then he settled down on the pavement and began to wrestle with something that looked very much like a cricket ball *en croute*.

I thought it best not to tell the café proprietor. He might have withdrawn his sponsorship and you don't snitch on your friends, do you?

CHAPTER TEN

She was playing with a leaf in the courtyard as I pushed open the wrought-iron gate. She was teasing the poor thing something awful. You could tell from its body language that it had just about had enough. Its veins were standing out.

'Don't be such a bully.'

She turned as she heard my voice and raced over to greet me. She had a quick sniff at my suitcase and then lay on her back, with her legs in the air, waiting to have her tummy rubbed.

'Oh for goodness' sake, Aileen. Whatever will the neighbours think?'

I made that bit up, but she was pleased to see me – which is more than you could say for the cats.

Thermal and Frink were on privet patrol in the front garden. They give the hedge a thorough going-over twice a day. They have to sort through every leaf, sniffing and sifting. It's a sort of fingerprint test for other cats' bladders and Frink is really getting the hang of it. She has the case history of every cat in the district on file in her head, in duplicate and triplicate, and better still, her eyes don't water any more.

Thermal still has to deal with the doings of the devious Denton because, being such a tall cat, he always aims too high up the hedge and a short kitten just can't cope with that sort of thing, but it's only a matter of time.

I know it's a serious business and you have to have your wits about you, but they could at least have come over and said hello.

'Hi there, I'm back.'

They ignored me completely. They knew I was there. Little things gave them away. Thermal sniffed at the same twig three times over and then Frink pretended to need a second opinion.

'*I'm not so sure about this one, Thermal.*'

'*Don't worry about that. It's one of mine.*'

'*Rather pleasant.*'

'*Thank you very much.*'

I tried again. I can be very firm when I have to be.

'I'm home.'

They stared at one another.

'*Did you hear something?*'

'*Take no notice. It's only that man.*'

'*What man is that?*'

'*You remember. The one who walked out on us years ago. Perhaps it was before your time. Just ignore him.*'

I thought, stuff them. I'll go and see what Tigger's up to, but I couldn't find her anywhere. Arthur was fast asleep on his pillow in the hall. I had only been away for a couple of days, but all the same I was surprised to see how old he looked.

A good deal of weight had fallen from his haunches and his bowed back legs reminded me of a catapult I once made out of a hazel branch. They were nothing more than a couple of twigs, when once they had been stout enough to provide all the power for his famous flying starts.

He didn't seem to be breathing. I knelt down beside him to see if there was any rise and fall in his body. I must have done this half a dozen times a day since he became ill, every time he dropped off to sleep.

Nothing seemed to be happening. I laid my hand on his shoulder and, right on cue, there came a deep purr as though from the bottom of a coal mine. Then one blurry eye fixed itself upon one of mine for a few seconds before taking cover once again.

'Did you have a nice time?'

'Yes, thank you, Arthur.'

'Good. You must tell me all about . . .'

'Well it was . . .'

'. . . one of these days.'

Aileen had placed a small pile of mail on my desk. I always enjoy this bit – when there are two or three days' supply all bundled up together. I feel like a wholesaler.

I always open the Jiffy bags first. Bad news very rarely comes trussed up in a Jiffy bag and more often than not those thick fluffy walls will be cosseting some new edition of one of my books in a foreign language, or maybe a library copy in large print.

It always gives me a kick to see a copy of *The Cat Who Came In From The Cold* all smartly dressed up in German as *Das Kätzchen das aus dem Regen kam*, or in Italian as *Il gatto che venne dal freddo*.

This time there were half a dozen copies of Jack Rosenthal's screenplay for the film *Wide-Eyed and Legless*, which he had adapted from my first book *Diana's Story*. Slim and glossy, they were to be aimed at the education market – colleges, schools and universities. I squeezed myself. Having left school with nothing more than a flea in my ear, I was now in danger of becoming a set subject.

The first small envelope I opened spilled a ten-pound note out onto my desk. I read the short note that had been laboriously printed on a sheet of ruled paper, torn from an exercise book.

'Thank you very much for trusting me. Here's your fiver back – and keep the change.'

I squeezed myself for the second time in as many minutes. My friend on the train had come up trumps, but I wished he had managed to keep the tip down to the bare 10 per cent.

Two or three bills followed and then came a letter from Tim Williamson, a young journalist friend of mine. He had filmed us for a video a few weeks ago and afterwards, over a glass of wine, had talked at some length about a witches' coven in Bradford.

When I first moved up to Huddersfield I never imagined I would come across any such thing as a gay Yorkshireman; not in my wildest dreams. It was something that only happened down south. I obviously hadn't thought it through, but the words 'gay' and 'Yorkshire' have always seemed to me to be a contradiction in terms.

'Eh, lad! You look right bonny in that flat cap and muffler. It's your colour is brown – will you give us a kiss?'

'Happen.'

The idea of there being a witches' coven in Bradford slipped neatly into the same category. I could cope with the idea of them cavorting naked on the moors of North Yorkshire, even more so the thought of them flitting in and out of the crumbling walls of Whitby Abbey at midnight, but not Bradford – not in a million years.

I thought there might be a story here for me. Tim and I would each tackle it in a different way. I had a vision of a string of young women cavorting naked outside a take-away curry house and the thought appealed to me.

He had promised to keep me posted, but his investigations seemed to have come to a dead end.

'They are proving to be rather elusive. I haven't managed to talk to any of the witches yet – but I have found the God of Fertility. He's a geography teacher from Keighley.'

Somehow it took all the magic out of it for me. The very idea of a God of Fertility with three biros sticking out of the top pocket of his Harris tweed hacking jacket, having to leave early because he has a great pile of marking to do – well it just didn't seem right somehow, so I decided to leave well alone.

Once I've been away for a few days I find it difficult to slip straight back into a writing mode. I need to get up and write and then go to bed and sleep and then get up and write again, day after day, week after week. Once I have had a glimpse of the outside world then I can't settle down to it and so I went downstairs and switched on the television in the kitchen.

Why are the adverts louder than the programmes? As soon as we come to a natural break, up goes the volume. If it's a crafty attempt to grab the viewers' attention then it fails miserably as far as I am concerned. First I switched the sound down and then I switched over to the BBC. Then I switched it down again.

I could hear another sound. That of a cat crying in the distance. I popped my head around the corner of the hall door, but Arthur was still fast asleep on his pillow.

There it was again. Rather muffled, sort of double-glazed, like a cat might sound if it were trying to throw its voice. I looked out of the kitchen window, but only the presence of Arthur's wire brush marred a rather pleasing landscape that had cost us an arm and a leg. Maybe the brush was a ventriloquist?

Wait a minute. It was coming from under the sink. No it wasn't – it was from over there. During the next few minutes I heard that damn cat crying in the airing cupboard, the knife drawer and the waste-disposal unit.

I sat down at the kitchen table, closed my eyes and tried to tune my ears in to the right direction. I have seen the cats do it – they have over twenty muscles in each ear, you know, and they can home them in independently.

I can't. I don't seem to have any muscles at all in my ears. So, with my eyes still tightly shut, I rotated my head like the gun turret of a Sherman tank, very slowly, round and round, until I began to feel quite dizzy.

I opened my eyes and kept absolutely still, but the kitchen kept going round. It swam in sections, each of them swaying before me, and in one of the sections there was a cat with a huge head, leering at me through the glass door of the washing-machine.

'Tigger!'

I raced over and pressed the button on the door. Nothing happened, and the huge head seemed to split in two as a vast mouth opened wide in protest. Those *teeth* – she looked about the size of a Bengal tiger.

I tried again, this time first switching on the power, and the door swung open and a disappointingly small cat jumped out.

'What on earth were you doing in there?'

She shook herself and then took refuge under a kitchen chair. In times of trouble she likes a roof over her head.

'It was that woman again.'

'Well, you know she can't see you.'

'I think it's time we had her put down.'

I knelt down and stroked her. She must have jumped in while Aileen was folding the washing. Or perhaps she had been washed and then tumbled dry. If so, Aileen had made a remarkably good job of her. She didn't even need ironing.

Tigger strolled over to the airing cupboard, reared up on her back legs and began to beat a tattoo on the door with her front paws.

This means, roughly translated – *I wish to go up there, on that little wooden shelf above the hot-water tank, so that I can relax for a few moments, well away from all the other cats and especially out of the way of that marauding woman who inadvertently sticks me in the washing-machine. So if you wouldn't mind placing your right hand under my bum and your left hand in such a position that it steadies me while still leaving my front paws free, you can then elevate me the necessary six feet or so and I will do the rest. I'll call you when I need you.*

'Do you want to go up there?'

'Oh, for God's sake, man – do you want it in writing?'

She clambered in and turned round three times before settling down on a pile of spare tablecloths. I left her to it and walked over to the television.

'Door.'

'Sorry.'

I picked up the bleeper and punched up the sound. The news was about to begin. Martyn Lewis cleared his throat and Moira Stuart's disapproving glance told him, in no uncertain manner, that he ought to have gone before the programme started. If they still pair newscasters according to their sexual chemistry, then these two must have slipped through the net. I poured myself another cup of coffee.

Through Channels One to Four the formula for presenting the news remains pretty much the same: this is what has happened – now let's see who we can blame. Only nine minutes gone and already three reputations had been hanged, drawn and quartered – those of a very small doctor from Pakistan, the entire management of Barclays Bank and a tattooed social worker who seemed to have cornered the market in bewilderment and now had it down to a fine art.

When will they realize that we are only human? We

are bound to make mistakes – that's what we human beings do. It's what we are best at. Why not adopt a more positive attitude?

'This morning, in Huddersfield, for the first time in his life, boyish author Deric Longden spelled the word "tattooed" correctly without first having to consult either his dictionary or his spell-check. Nice one, Deric.'

The kitchen doorbell burst into life. It's a fine old clockwork bell, as old as the house itself and still as enthusiastic as ever. At the slightest touch it goes berserk, whirring round and round, fluttering the lino tiles and setting teeth on edge at a hundred paces.

The airing cupboard door shot open and Tigger's face pushed its way past a single brown sock that had been hanging there for ages, waiting for the divorce to come through. Her fur panicked and stood on end.

'*For God's sake, make it stop!*'

If you don't get there in time the casing flies off the bell and it's the very devil to get back on. I caught it in mid-air and opened the door.

Our plumber has been known to smile once in a while, but it takes it out of him and he likes to save his energy for the job in hand, so he just gave me one of his nods as he padded on past me into the kitchen.

'I know where it is.'

'Hang on.'

I chased after him and caught him in the hall.

'You'll have to wait for a moment. I think Aileen is in there.'

I led him back into the kitchen and tried to sit him

down, but he preferred to stand and so we stood.

'She won't be a minute.'

She wasn't. There came the sound of a distant flush and then the kitchen door burst open and Aileen charged in, brandishing the cardboard tube from a defunct toilet roll in her right hand.

'Right, you bastard – you asked for it.'

And with that she pulled out the pin with her teeth and hurled the cardboard tube across the room before flinging herself full length, face down on the kitchen floor, her hands over her ears and her forehead pressed hard against the shaggy pile of the eight-sided rug.

The plumber and I watched in silence as the un-exploded tube rolled menacingly over towards the airing cupboard, coming to rest a foot from the skirting-board. Tigger stared down from the top shelf, her head peeping out between two yellow dusters drying on the short line.

Any other day of the week I would have joined in the game and thrown myself full length on the floor, covering the lethal device with my own body, thus saving both my unstable wife and my faithful cat from horrendous injuries. But not today.

'Aileen – the plumber's here.'

She lay quite still for a moment or two before rising slowly to her feet and dusting herself down. Then, with the cool and nonchalant charm for which she is so rightly famous, she beckoned the plumber to follow her out into the hall.

'It's this way.'

He hesitated slightly and then fell in behind her. At the kitchen door he paused and turned towards me, his eyes pleading.

'You are coming as well – aren't you?'

They didn't need me. I sat down at the table and zapped up the news with the remote control. Martyn and Moira were getting stuck into some building society or other and a man in a grey suit was explaining that it all belonged to us really and they were only looking after our best interests. I quite liked him but you could tell he wasn't Moira's sort. She dismissed him abruptly, her eyes as cold as ice and her lips as thin as paper.

Martyn Lewis was shot down in flames not so long ago when he launched a campaign for more good news on television. It would never work. Even if the BBC served up nothing but a daily diet of heart-warming stories, each as light and frothy as a soufflé, so long as Moira Stuart is there to pass on the news to a waiting nation we could never be quite sure whether it was good news or bad. With her buttoned-down delivery she can make winning the National Lottery sound like a four-mile tailback on the M62.

Aileen swayed past me, her hip brushing my elbow, sending a table-mat and a large Jaffa orange spinning through 360 degrees.

'OK?'

She didn't answer. She pushed on through the kitchen door and out into the courtyard. I could see her through the window, walking as though in a trance. She came to a halt by the wire brush and then, taking hold of a great bunch of hair in either hand, she threw back her head and yelled.

'Aaaaaaaaaargh!'

At least he is the sort of plumber who doesn't like to hang about. Within minutes he had sorted out the shower, fixed the loose handle on the toilet and removed £32.50 from my wallet without going anywhere near it. I admired him.

We popped in and out of the shower room several times during the next half-hour, just to flush the toilet. For the past month or so we had been pressing down gently and then letting go. This would be followed by two quick pumps and a hold down, then a slow release and finally a combined press, twist and jerk with double axel.

It was a nightmare when visitors called. They were hardly likely to be in a position where I could stand over them and talk them through it, so I had had to run off a thick pile of instructions on the photocopier and hand them each a sheet of A4 paper whenever they asked where the smallest room was.

It was only a partial success. The twist and jerk threw most of them and the length of the hold-down was crucial and rather difficult to put into words. It depended on how long it took for the water in the pan to look lively and bubble up. If it just sat there all flat and lifeless, then you had to start all over again. I could go on, but I won't.

And so we rejoiced as we flushed and the sound of pounding water was to be heard all over the house. Thermal and Frink came in from the garden to see what all the fuss was about.

'*Is it working again?*'

'Yes.'

'*Oh good . . .*'

Thermal hooked his paws over the seat and peered down into the pan.

'*Give it a quick flush for me.*'

Would you believe it? After treating me like dirt, out there by the privet hedge. I brought the lid down and nearly took his head off.

'Aileen. There are a couple of cats in the shower room. They want me to flush the toilet for them.'

She popped her head around the door.

'Is Tigger there? She hasn't been around since I did the washing first thing this morning.'

'No. It's not Tigger,' I told her as I put my arm around her shoulders and escorted her back into the hall. 'I have no idea who they are. I have never seen those two cats before in my life.'

A U T U M N

CHAPTER ELEVEN

It was to be in full colour, she had said. The photographer would be the first to arrive and she would follow on later – she couldn't be doing with interruptions once she had an interview up and running.

'Mind you – they're a breed apart, photographers. He'll probably go and get himself run over on the way there.'

So what to wear? I had already gone through my wardrobe half a dozen times. I had tried this with that and that with this, matching colours that would have had Van Gogh screaming in his sleep. Aileen couldn't understand what all the fuss was about.

'Wear your green silk shirt and a pair of jeans.'

'That's what I was wearing when I came up to get changed.'

123

'There you are then.'

I shovelled everything back in the wardrobe and did as I was told. It's all to do with insecurity of course, I couldn't imagine Alan Bennett getting in such a flap. Thora Hird once told me that he had arrived for a meeting in a Crombie overcoat that he'd bought from a charity shop on the way there. It was two sizes too large for him and long enough to keep his feet warm.

'What do you think, Thora?'

'It's very nice. It'd look lovely on somebody else.'

I took a sly glance in the mirror on the way downstairs, pulled in my stomach and went and sat in the lounge to wait.

I think the photographer must have got himself run over. He was half an hour late already, so I settled back in the easy chair and began to nod off. Thermal came over to join me.

'Are we friends again?'

'Go on then.'

He jumped up on my knee and we did a little bonding. He stared at me and I stared at him, opening and closing our eyes alternately and purring. I must be getting better at purring, it doesn't seem to embarrass him any more.

He fell asleep first and I joined him soon after. I have no idea how long we slept but we were still out cold when the door burst open and Aileen charged into the room, followed by a rather flustered photographer and a journalist who looked none too pleased to be in his company.

'And this is my husband.'

I leapt to my feet and I'd like to say that Thermal followed suit. I'm sure he would have done if he could, but he just happened to have one of his claws caught in the top of my zip.

He hung there for a moment or two, suspended in mid-air by one paw, and then very slowly he abseiled down the outside of my trousers, taking my zip down with him as he went.

If you have ever been to the circus and admired the grace with which the trapeze artiste slides down that rope after she has finished her act – well she wasn't a patch on Thermal. He should have done so to a rapturous round of applause, instead of which he landed on the hearthrug in the middle of an embarrassed silence and then I had to kneel down and try to untangle him from my zip.

It took ages. With my fly wide open and the cat wide-eyed with panic I had to be really firm with him. I trapped his little body in between my legs, jammed his head up against the front of the settee, and then went to work on his claw.

It was really stuck. It had gone through the hole in that little tab that dangles from the top of the zip and while I was trying to get it out he was trying to mark me for life with however many claws he had left.

God knows how I got it out but I managed it somehow and Thermal fled from the room with his head down low and his tail held high. I got to my feet, zipped myself up, and then, with as much dignity as I could possibly muster, limped over to greet my guests with my hand outstretched.

'So glad you could come.'

With some journalists the little episode would have broken the ice, but this one seemed to have been frozen at birth.

'Huddersfield? You want me to go to Huddersfield?'

She would have insisted on a series of injections

before she set out on such a journey and my wrestling match with Thermal only seemed to confirm her suspicions that she had arrived in the back of beyond.

After an hour or so of answering question after question and trying very hard to dodge those questions that had a certain spin on them it was a pleasure to be able to wave her off, slumped in the back of the oldest taxi in town. She didn't wave back, or at least I don't think she did. I wasn't able to see clearly through the giant cloud of exhaust fumes that followed the pair of them down the road.

I needed some fresh air, so after patting my pocket to check for loose change I made my way up to the garage for a packet of cigarettes. Smoking is good for me. Walking up to the garage for a packet of cigarettes is the only exercise I get. An old lady stood dithering on the edge of the pavement, her purse clutched in her hand and her eyes fixed on a line of traffic that seemed to be coming from another world entirely, a world about which she knew nothing.

'Shall we go across together?'

I kept an eye on the island down the road. Pawing the ground in a side-street, a huge car transporter seemed to be having much the same trouble as the old lady. Neither of them was all that nippy. The lorry carried eight brand-new saloons on its back. The old lady had some eighty years on hers and she held on to my arm almost as firmly as she held on to the precious purse in her hand.

A learner driver stalled on the island and the transporter made a break for it. The old lady's fingers dug deeper into my arm and we sauntered across the road, while down at the island a long line of cars fretted and fumed.

'We used to keep turkeys,' she remarked.

'Did you?'

'Busy life.'

'I bet it was.'

We had a bit of trouble with the steps to the garage forecourt and then she tried to go into the shop through a plate-glass window. I pushed the door open and she saw the sense in it.

'Bet you miss it, don't you?'

'What?'

'The turkeys.'

She tagged onto the end of the queue and waited patiently for her turn. She looked so old and fragile.

'Not really. They're as thick as shit, turkeys.'

There didn't seem much else to say after that. The other people in the queue suddenly became very interested in the goods around them. They closely examined little sachets of windscreen cleaner, reading the instructions on the back, before browsing their way through the A to Z maps of Bradford and Keighley, ears cocked for further revelations.

They were to be disappointed. The girl on the till was very efficient and before long we had worked our way up to the front.

The old lady tipped the contents of her purse out onto the counter, a rather miserable collection of coins from before we went decimal, some from after we went decimal and some I didn't recognize at all. There was a big button and a little button and a grey Polo mint that had a lump of fluff jammed in the middle of the hole.

'Have I got enough for ten Regal Extra?'

The girl separated the collection into three piles; old coins in one, new coins in another, buttons and Polo mint and the lump of fluff in a special pile of their own, together with a fur-covered Spangle that had refused to budge at the first time of asking.

'Not quite, love – you're ten pence short.'

'Oh dear.'

The old lady didn't hang about. She pushed the debris up to one end of the counter and then began shovelling it back in her purse.

We couldn't have this. I dug my hand in my pocket.

'Here – let me.'

The girl behind the counter flashed me a warning glance.

'But I'd like to . . .'

She shook her head and waited until the old lady had shuffled off up to the other end of the shop. Then she leaned over the counter and whispered confidentially.

'She doesn't even smoke.'

I was out of my depth here. I hung around while she served another customer.

'She comes in and asks for ten Regal Extra. We count her money and she never has enough – it's always the same purse. I don't think she uses it for anything else.'

She swiped a credit card through the machine and pressed a number of buttons. The till whirred and the customer signed.

'Now she feels like a proper customer so she can hang around for an hour or so and read all the news-papers and magazines.'

I glanced out of the corner of my eye. The old lady had propped herself up against the cold cabinet and was relaxing with *Woman's Realm*, her lips tracing out the words as her eyes travelled slowly down the page.

'If you had given her that ten pence you would have really buggered things up.'

I shouted goodbye as I left the shop, but she didn't seem to hear me. It didn't matter – I was back in the real world again where you find kindness in the strangest of disguises and it suited me down to the ground.

I walked back through the park, mulling over the interview and wondering how many more times I could tell the same old stories without boring everyone to death.

The reporter had asked what first started me off writing and I had told her about the BBC short story competition.

'You had to use a pen name, so I called myself biro.'

But it all started a long time before that. I remember my first rejection. I was a hard-hitting twelve-year-old who had just had his eyes opened by reading *Animal Farm* and was determined to carve out a career for himself as a writer. I worked hard for several weeks, researching and refining my material, polishing my prose until it shone bright purple. This was some article, so important that it deserved lots and lots of exclamation marks, and I made sure to leave plenty of space at the end of every other sentence so that I could put them in later.

I decided to offer the first British serial rights to the school magazine and dropped my masterpiece in at their office one afternoon. A few days later the headmaster sent for me, and the whys and wherefores of such an invitation fluttered about in my head as I waited outside his study. Did they give the Nobel Prize for Literature to twelve-year-old kids?

'You can go in now.'

He had my article on his desk and a scowl on his face. The scowl had been there for as long as I could remember. He wore it like a balaclava – his mother must have knitted it for him when he was a child and she had dropped a few stitches here and there.

He read in silence for a while and then tapped the wad of handwritten pages with a bony finger. I had made a wise decision in my choice of paper – feint-ruled lines and a margin on the left; it looked most professional.

'Did you really write this?'

'Yes, sir.'

And with no help whatsoever. My mother had checked the spelling with the help of my Uncle Len's dictionary, but apart from that it was all my own work and my mother thought it was brilliant.

He turned the title over on his tongue once or twice before finally spitting it out.

'"The Art Of Embalming".'

I had briefly considered using 'Undertaking – A Dying Art'. In fact I think I still preferred it in many ways, but my mother said she thought it was a bit on the jokey side and we had agreed that 'The Art Of Embalming' had a certain ring about it.

'Putrefaction?'

'Yes, sir.'

He placed his fingertips together and put them to his nose.

'And where on earth did you learn about putrefaction?'

From my grandfather as it happened. He came alive when he talked about putrefaction. He would lay down his pipe on the kitchen table and lean into his subject, citing case histories from his early days when undertaking was a job for a real man, not like what it was nowadays. He was very strong on decomposition as well.

'Bodily fluids?'

My grandfather could go on for hours about bodily fluids, it was all a matter of where to start really. When I had to go and stay with my grandparents for the weekend the silences would be long and torturous. The only way to kick-start him into some sort of a conversation was to bring up either bodily fluids or chrysanthemums and to be honest I had had it up to here with his blessed chrysanthemums.

The headmaster gave a slight shudder.

'These worms that are supposed to come and eat you up – at Old Brampton of all places.'

Ah yes, the worms. Now they had taken a bit of writing about. I had shown great courage in mentioning them at all. The nightmares had come thick and fast ever since and I had got around to thinking that maybe I shouldn't have gone into it in such detail. A writer has to suffer for his art, but there are limits.

The scowl sank further and further down his face until it was almost sitting on his shoulders.

'My mother was buried at Old Brampton – ten years ago.'

There wouldn't be much left of her by now, I thought, but I didn't say anything.

He was quiet for a time. Just sat there staring at a space above my head, his two forefingers tapping on the end of his nose as though he were playing the recorder. I hate silences and I have to fill them. Perhaps I had gone too far with those worms, what with his mother and all. Fortunately he stepped smartly into the breach.

'And what's all this about a motorbike and side-car?'

Now that was where I had brought my father into the story for a little light relief, which was something that didn't happen to him all that often.

When my mother read the first draft she felt that there was something missing, but she just couldn't put her finger on it, so she read it over and over again and eventually she said that it wouldn't do any harm at all if I added a touch of humour. She said it needed lightening up a little.

I suggested that we went back to the original title but she said no, it could do with something more than that. And then, as though we had been reading each other's thoughts, we came up with the motorbike and side-car.

You see, when my father had to go and pick up a body there were one or two things he had to weigh up first. Was it worth taking the hearse or not? Had the deceased left enough to pay for a proper funeral or had they gone and died on the parish? If the latter was the case then it didn't do to make too much of a fuss. It was far better to remove the body discreetly – no point in building up the deceased's hopes, making him think he was going to get brass handles and all the paraphernalia of a proper funeral. Besides, it kept the mileage down on the hearse.

So my father had this side-car made. It was the same shape as a coffin, but without that voluptuous curve at the hip. You slid the coffin in at the back end, through a little door that fastened with a hook and eye. More often than not he could manoeuvre the bike up a side passage and take the deceased out through the back door of the house. That way you didn't have all the neighbours standing around gawping.

On one occasion he was called out to deal with an old man who lived on his own. The best part of a week had gone by before the neighbours found him, sitting up in a rocking-chair in the front room. His body had set in that position, so my father had to break several bones before he could fit him into the side-car. He told the story often and I knew it off by heart.

'It would have been a damn sight easier to have sat him on the back of the bike.'

It always caused a laugh at family get togethers, so I had slipped it into my article – just to lighten things up a little.

The headmaster coughed. It was a dry sort of cough that always spelt trouble when it crept up behind you in the playground.

He was reading the bit about the accident now. My mother had told me that this was bound to be a sure-fire winner.

There were times when it wasn't all that convenient for my father to pop down to the workshop first to pick up an empty coffin, and on those occasions the body would be slipped straight into the side-car, without the added comfort of a wooden overcoat. Sometimes he wouldn't even think of taking a coffin, if he happened to be picking up a customer from a workhouse or some other such institution where grieving relatives were unlikely to be thick on the ground.

Late one night, as my father was driving along with a body in the side-car, a dog ran out across Chatsworth Road and my father slammed on the brakes. The little door at the back flew open and the body shot out into the road.

A farmer from Wadshelf was following on behind in his van and he could hardly believe his eyes. He'd run right over the deceased before he knew where he was and afterwards he just sat there in his cab, staring straight ahead. They say he was never quite the same after that.

My mother said that if the farmer had reported the accident to the police then that would have been the end of the business, but fortunately he decided not to take the matter any further – apparently it was something to do with what he had in the back of his van at the time.

I waited for the headmaster's seal of approval. I knew that my article was a little on the long side, but I was prepared to make cuts if he insisted. In fact I had done so already. I had left out the art of embalming entirely – just kept the title because it had a ring to it.

It hadn't been an easy decision to make. My mother always made sure that I was well out of the way when there was any embalming going on, but my grandfather had filled me in on the details and only recently I had managed to grab a brief glimpse of the process.

My mother had to take some paperwork over to a rival undertaker – there had been some minor disaster or other and the two firms were sharing the workload. She left me in the main hall while she went about her business and after a while I got bored and opened a door. A man stood with his back to me and a body lay on a white tiled table. The man was pumping away vigorously at a small wooden handle, backwards and forwards, keeping a watchful eye on a glass container that hung from a bracket on the wall above his head.

Underneath the table stood a chrome bucket on a pair of wooden blocks. We had a bucket like that. It was just the way my grandfather had described it to me.

'You pump the fluid in and it pushes the blood out. It's quite simple really. The art is in adding the colouring so that the deceased looks as well as he did the day before he took ill. You can't have him looking too healthy, though, it worries the relatives. Never been able to understand that myself.'

I walked over towards the table, to introduce myself. The man swung round and shouted at me.

'Bugger off.'

Another man came in and took me away. Then they made me stand outside the front door until my mother had finished her business. So much for the brotherhood.

The headmaster stood up and walked over to the window, taking my precious pages with him. To be honest I think he overreacted. Of course, I knew that my article wasn't likely to be everyone's cup of tea, but I was trying to break down barriers here and I would have expected more from a man of letters.

He tore them up in front of me. First in half and then almost in half again, but the bulk proved too much for him.

'Just go away and we'll forget all about it.'

Well he might have done, but I haven't.

CHAPTER TWELVE

Working on the play about my mother meant that I had to spend the next couple of weeks digging deep into my past. I even read *Lost For Words* twice over, and wading through one of your own books isn't something I would recommend – there was so much I wanted to pull out and write all over again.

I have a drawer in my filing cabinet devoted entirely to stories about my mother. It's divided into two sections: 'Virgin' at the front for unused material and 'Deflowered' at the rear for those pieces that have been drafted into use in various books and radio broadcasts.

I am afraid my mother isn't much of a virgin any-more. Most of the stuff had worked its way round to the back. Just a few odd scraps of paper floated about in the virgin territory, but one of them brought with it a wry smile and the antiseptic whiff of the hospital waiting-room.

Two words – that's all – written on the back of a National Health pamphlet on venereal disease. In typical Sixties style the overall message of the pamphlet was that while they were rather disgusted with you for picking it up in the first place they were prepared to have a look and see what they could do about it – which is fair enough I suppose. If I were a doctor I would be far happier tinkering around with the ears, nose and throat. I would take on a lad and train him up and then he could look after anything that went wrong below the waist.

I had no personal interest in the contents myself, you understand. I gave it a quick flip through because there was nothing else to read. I smoothed the pamphlet out on my desk and the bitter-sweet memories came flooding back.

It must have been just after midnight in Chesterfield's Royal Infirmary. For the umpteenth time my first wife Diana had collapsed and had to be rushed into the emergency ward. We had been staying overnight at my mother's house and she insisted on coming along to keep me company.

We moped around, feeling helpless as usual, waiting to see that Diana was settled down and comfortable before we called it a day and left for home.

The waiting-room was like a barn. A cheerless place, hung with ancient anaglypta that had long since given up the ghost, suffocated beneath a dozen coats of magnolia gloss. What wasn't now a dirty yellow was coated in a ghastly green. Or was it brown? I can't remember – but I do know that my mother said it reminded her of where Nellie Elliot used to live.

'They had a dildo rail running right round the room.'

I never looked at Nellie Elliot in quite the same way after that, but I suspect my mother had it wrong. She was a dab hand at that sort of thing.

A pair of double doors swung open at the far end of the room and a porter reversed in, pulling a wheelchair behind him. The woman in it was obviously in considerable pain. Her face was drawn and she held her hand to her side. The porter placed the wheelchair opposite my mother and then went off to attend to other things.

We were sitting on a couple of chairs that had been specially upholstered in natural plastic. They had high backs and no arms, and were the kind that curve up at the front so that you can see right up old ladies' skirts.

As I rose to my feet the plastic came up with me as though it couldn't bear to let me go, and then as we parted company there came the gentle sound of breaking wind. I sat down and stood up again, repeating the process so that they wouldn't think it was me.

The woman, still holding her side, leaned forward in her chair and took my mother into her confidence. With her suffering written all over her face she whispered, 'Renal Colic.'

My mother didn't hesitate. She sat up as best she could and stuck out her hand in welcome.

'Annie Longden,' she said. 'Pleased to meet you.'

Across the room I took out my pen and wrote the words 'renal colic' on the back of the pamphlet as the porter returned for his patient. After they had gone my mother came over to join me by the window.

'She must be French with a name like that,' she said.

* * *

I tucked my mother away in the filing cabinet and went to lock up for the night. Before I could do that I had to find the cats and then shuffle them around so that they would be where I would expect them to be first thing in the morning.

Frink was already fast asleep in the cellar, curled up in her tea cosy. She's still only a kitten and I like her to have her full eight hours, even though she gets at least another ten during the day.

Arthur was flat out on his pillow by the radiator. I brought his litter tray up with me from the cellar and placed it where he would fall over it if he went walk-about in the middle of the night. It's not that I don't trust him, it's just that now he isn't getting around so well I feel happier if he's living *en suite*.

Tigger was up in the airing cupboard and had been for most of the day. She opened one eye as I opened the door.

'*Do you mind?*'

'Sorry.'

But I couldn't find Thermal anywhere. In fact I hadn't seen him since he had complained about the menu at teatime. He likes his tuna in brine and I had inadvertently bought him a tin of tuna in spring water. He said it didn't have the same bite to it and told me to watch out and be more careful in the future. I told him not to be so cheeky or I would sort him out once and for all, and he had said you and whose army.

We had made it up afterwards, we always do.

'*It was quite pleasant really. Made a nice change.*'

'I'm sorry – I should have noticed.'

'*Don't worry about it. We all make mistakes.*'

He had given me a quick bump with his rump on my ankle, and I had scratched the back of his neck and then let his tail run through my fingers as he walked away. It's what life is all about.

Then Frink came over and told me that Thermal had eaten her bowl of Kitten Whiskas and that she was starving to death. So I gave her the saucer of tuna in spring water, which had hardly been touched. Frink ate every last mouthful, but then told me not to bother buying any more – she said it didn't have the same bite to it. Sometimes I wonder why I bother.

I stood on the doorstep and called Thermal but he didn't seem to be around, so I gave up on him and started worrying about Aileen instead. If he was locked out he could always use the cat flap in the cellar, but Aileen wouldn't even get her head through it.

I found her in the bathroom and as I pushed open the door the Taiwanese lady who lives in her talking watch told me that the time was now 1.15 a.m. She's very reliable. She updates the time every quarter of an hour in a clear crisp lisp and she is slowly driving me mad.

The man in the shop twiddled with one of the buttons the day we bought it and we have never found out how to make it stop. Aileen doesn't mind – it keeps her posted as the day flies by, but it sets my teeth on edge.

So at night we shut the watch away in the bathroom, under the cushion on the cane chair with all the towels piled on top. With luck she might suffocate.

I had switched the electric blanket on about an hour before, and so as my feet slid smoothly under the duvet it was a very warm cat that bit my toe. I was too tired to sort him out, so I let him stay where he was and he purred and forgave me for waking him and after a while he crept up the bed and slept between us, bum to bum to bum.

The three of us slept like a log for at least five minutes and then, through a dense fog, I heard the Taiwanese lady clearing her throat.

'It's one forty-five a.m.'

Thermal came up the bed like a train out of a tunnel.

'What was that?'

'It's all right, don't worry. It's only Aileen's watch.'

He snuggled back down between us.

'I knew this was going to be a mistake.'

I lay there for a while, trying to recreate the sound in my head. It seemed to come from over on the dressing-table. Aileen must have brought the watch with her when she came out of the bathroom. I find thinking very tiring and I must have dropped off to sleep again.

'It's two a.m.'

This time Aileen was the first to react. She rolled over towards me.

'What was that?'

'It's your watch. You must have brought it in with you.'

She groaned and laid her head on my chest.

'I shan't get off again now.'

A rather flat cat stuck out a limp paw and scratched at my navel.

'Tell her. For God's sake tell her.'

'I think you're lying on Thermal, love.'

I decided to put the watch out of its misery while the other two made it up and I would have done had I been able to find it. It certainly wasn't on the dressing-table.

'Where did you put it?'

'I told you. I can't even remember bringing it in with me.'

I searched everywhere, even dipping into Aileen's dressing-gown pocket, which I thought showed great initiative.

'It wouldn't be there.'

'It might have been.'

I slipped back under the duvet and we pluffed up the pillows, the three of us sitting straight-backed against the headboard, waiting with ears cocked so that we could pinpoint her position when she told us that it was now 2.15 a.m.

'It's two fifteen a.m.'

'Where was that?'

'The wardrobe.'

I pulled open the door and a solid wall of well-bred separates blinked at the light and shuffled at the intrusion.

'What were you wearing today?'

'You mean you never noticed?'

'Just tell me.'

If she had been hiding in there then she must have heard me coming and made a break for it, so I made a pot of tea and we sat up in bed once more and waited for her to tell us when it was 2.30 a.m.

It seemed like ages and Aileen thought she must have called it a day.

'It's not time yet,' I told her.

'It must be,' she said, and to prove her point automatically bent her arm and pressed the little button on her talking watch that had been strapped to her wrist all this time. Even the Taiwanese lady sounded somewhat embarrassed.

'It's two twenty-eight a.m.'

I marched her off to the bathroom in disgrace, thinking that I should have done this with Aileen still attached. I stuffed her under the cushion and then stacked a pile of towels on top. She muttered something about it being 2.30 a.m. as I closed the door on her and told her to go and get knotted. I had to be up in four hours' time.

As things turned out I didn't even manage that. If you ever decide to break into somebody's house may I suggest that you do so around five-thirty in the morning. It's very effective. Your victims will be fast asleep, half-baked and quite possibly naked.

There's also a chance that they might have a cat with them in the bedroom, in which case the man of the house will probably trip over it and fall flat on his face as he leaps out of bed.

The sound of shattering glass cut through the silence of the morning air. Then the front door burst open, grinding shards of glass and lumps of lead against the mosaic-tiled flooring in the outer hall. I heard feet pounding and then the alarm bells went off and filled the house from top to bottom.

Thermal must have heard all this long before we did because he was up and about and charging around the room. I went head over heels over the top of him, but I must have bounced nicely because I was back on my feet in no time at all.

We sleep downstairs, right by the front door, which now stood wide open. The intruders had smashed a rock through one of the stained-glass panels. A hundred years it had been there, built to last by some anonymous craftsman who had fashioned it with enormous skill and a bucketful of pride. And now, in a few brief seconds, it had been shattered to smithereens by some cretin who didn't even know the meaning of the word.

Was he still in the house? I went back into the bedroom, to see if Aileen was all right and to put on a pair of trousers.

'What's happening?'

'We've had a break-in.'

'Have they gone?'

'I don't know. You ring the police and I'll have a look round.'

She picked up the bedside telephone and began to dial. I pulled the bedroom door shut behind me and went out into the hall.

'Aileen.'

'Yes.'

'Slip the bolt on.'

At least Arthur wasn't letting the intrusion interfere with the more important things in life. He would have been fast asleep on his pillow, no more than six feet away, when the door burst open and he was still lying there when I came out to investigate. Now he was sitting bolt upright in his litter tray, having a crap. He has style, does Arthur.

I combed the house from top to bottom, pulling open wardrobe doors, looking under beds and behind the larger pieces of furniture. I had picked up a weapon on my way through the kitchen and I must have looked a fearsome sight with my bare chest, bare feet and baggy trousers. They would have known I really meant business, however, the moment they laid eyes on the vicious-looking milk pan I carried in my right hand.

I looked everywhere but there was no-one around and strangely enough they didn't seem to have taken anything with them. In fact they had penetrated no further than the outer hall. Maybe Arthur had frightened them off.

Aileen was dressed and crunching about on the broken glass by the time I came downstairs.

'Be careful,' I warned her.

'Bastards,' she said.

I have never been more proud of her. It's bad enough if you can see what's going on. The aftershock of a robbery is quite overwhelming and that feeling of security that you once took for granted has now gone for ever. The fact that you are so vulnerable stays with you for a long time to come, especially if you can't see past the end of your nose. But she was more angry than frightened.

'They are not going to ruin my life.'

The police came and went. They did their best, but they had another two calls on the radio in the short time they were with us and I had the feeling that they were somewhat overwhelmed.

'And you are sure they didn't take anything?'

'Not that we can see.'

'Well let us know if you find anything missing.'

We cleared up the mess and I made us a pot of coffee. Aileen reached for her cigarettes only to find that the packet was empty.

'Have one of mine.'

'No, it's all right. I've got a fresh packet.'

I pushed my chair back from the table.

'Whereabouts?'

'In my handbag. It's hanging up on the coat rack in the outer hall.'

It was a pretty stupid place to keep it I suppose, but it was so handy. She could pick it up as she went out and slip it back on the hook when she came back in. It's essential, when you can't see properly, that everything should have its own place and the place for her handbag was on the coat rack in the outer hall.

I remembered, a few days earlier, two men knocking at the front door and asking if I knew some girl or other. She was a student, they said, and she lived in a flat round here. One of them had hung on chatting as the other drifted away, long after I had convinced them that I had never heard of her in my life. His eyes had wandered past me on into the hall and I had felt uncomfortable. The two had exchanged a series of glances which, with hindsight, I was now able to decipher.

'Leave it. We can come back any time.'

Aileen assumed the role of repairmaster general. She's good at that, far better than I am. I get embarrassed. Halfway through a phone call to the insurance company I know for sure that they think I have ripped up the paving-stones myself and sold them to the highest bidder, and then a blush begins to spread all over my voice and I hear myself telling them not to worry, we'll sort it out ourselves.

I am just as bad with estimates.

'Now are you sure you can manage it at that. I don't want you to be out of pocket.'

So Aileen won't let me anywhere near them. She's mean and hard and yet somehow both the insurers and the contractors fall over themselves to please her.

By lunch-time she had cancelled the credit cards and contacted the bank and the insurance company. She had found a wonderful young man who was just as good with stained-glass panels as Michelangelo was with ceilings. Another man was already fitting dead-locks to all the outer doors and I was trying to reset the burglar alarm.

I know I paint a rather depressing picture of myself, but I do so with deadly accuracy. You see I am numerically dyslexic. I can't remember numbers. Give me a pen and a piece of paper and I can even work out my royalty statements, but I have no idea what the date is today, even though I looked it up in my diary less than five minutes ago.

It's the same with road numbers when I am travelling. I have become a dab hand at finding the M1, but then when I have to turn off onto the A427 at Junction 20 my mind turns into instant whip and I need a cup of coffee at Leicester Forest East service station to stop my hand from trembling.

In an attempt to find a suitable user code for the burglar alarm we had decided that my year of birth might be just the thing, I could hardly forget that. But only a couple of days ago I raced into the house and, with the beeper becoming more and more impatient with me, I stood in front of the panel – my mind a blank.

'Aileen. When was I born?'

'1936.'

'Thank you.'

(In case anyone with an interest in house clearances happens to be reading this, then I must tell you that we have now changed the number. I can't remember what it is.)

So Aileen called in a proper man to deal with the burglar alarm, which meant I was able to sit down and help her as she listed the contents of her handbag.

'Wallet containing cash, credit cards, cheque book . . .'

Those are the sort of items that first spring to mind. The mobile phone, the car keys, the house keys: they all spell trouble and financial loss. But a few weeks later they will be replaced and forgotten. There are others that never will.

'That silver toothpick you bought me in Dubai. Photos of the children when they were little. My mother's ring I was taking to be repaired. Oh God, my address book.'

We listed twenty-seven different items from her make-up bag – and I had always thought she was a natural beauty. She told me the prices and believe me it's cheaper to have the car serviced.

'There's my folding white stick, of course.'

I hoped that their consciences might take a nasty turn when they came across that, but I doubt it.

'My folding magnifying glass and my Parker pen. Damn it – my tape recorder. I'd forgotten about that, it had all my notes on it.'

'What about your disabled badge?'

'I've already seen to that.'

The list went on and on. Two pages of foolscap paper and we added to it constantly over the next few days. I thought about the two men who had called at the door and I was sure it must have been them. Why couldn't I remember what they looked like? One was short and the other tall and that was about it.

'I think he must have had an accomplice with him, Aileen.'

'Why's that?'

'He would never have been able to carry your handbag all on his own.'

She was wonderful. Never once did she let it upset her. Angry yes, but never a sign of nerves, and when I announced that I had to be away for a couple of nights later that week she took the news in her stride.

'I shall enjoy being on my own for a while.'

Then the following weekend we were having a cup of coffee at the Queen's Hotel in Leeds. We must have been in and out of every dress shop in the town centre. How she knows where they are I can't imagine. I certainly don't tell her. She can smell a silk jacket at a hundred paces.

I filled her cup from the cafetière and then added a dash of milk. She reached down and began to rifle through her brand-new handbag. We had found an identical replacement and so her fingers were able to go straight to one of those zippy little compartments that line the inside. She felt around for a while and then her face just fell apart.

'Oh, no.'

'What on earth's the matter?'

Whatever it was it was serious. This was the first time her defences had slipped in this way and I steeled myself for the bad news. She had another scout around in her handbag and then leaned over the table towards me.

'They pinched my sweeteners.'

CHAPTER THIRTEEN

The news of our burglary whipped through the neighbourhood like a forest fire, mainly because I insisted on telling the whole story to any man, woman or child who was prepared to stand still long enough and listen.

'You were lucky you know. The Faulkners lost everything. When they came back off holiday it had all gone.'

I didn't give a toss about the Faulkners. I had just had my front door kicked in and I wanted my share of the glory.

'They tied Mrs Rushworth to a chair, you know. She was there all night.'

Stuff Mrs Rushworth. She probably deserved everything she got. I only stopped these people so that I could tell them how, in the early hours of Friday morning and armed with nothing more than a milk pan, I set about four burly intruders and sent them packing.

'Mr Carisbrooke did that and he must be eighty if he's a day.'

You can't win. Eventually I stopped talking about it and then people would come up to me, trying to prise the story from between my sealed lips.

'I hear you chased 'em right up the M62.'

'Only as far as Hull.'

Then, just as I was getting into my stride, we had a bank robbery up in the village and within no time at all I was yesterday's news, fit only for wrapping around a greasy pile of fish and chips.

I didn't hear about it until it was all over. Apparently the police thought the robbers might still be holed up in the bank, when in fact they had long since fled the scene. But they couldn't take any chances, so they shut off the main street and put on one hell of a show, starring several live marksmen and a helicopter.

The helicopter hovered over the bank for the best part of an hour and the guns were trained on the main doors. And it was at the height of the seige that the village witnessed one of the great heroic acts of our time.

Nell works in Natural Choice, a few doors down, and she had no idea what was going on. So she strolled out of the shop and across the street with a carrier bag in either hand, thinking it was quiet for the time of day or at least that it would have been if it hadn't been for that bloody helicopter playing silly buggers over the bank.

When she came across the policeman all kitted out in battle gear, lying on his stomach in the middle of the pedestrian crossing with his gun pointing at the bank door, she had to take a slight detour around him – you know, like you do. She was only halfway across when a police officer with a loud hailer bawled at her from the comparative safety of a shop doorway.

'Go back, go back. You can't cross there.'

'Don't be ridiculous,' she shouted at him, waving her carrier bags in the air. 'I've got stuff for my freezer in here.'

I heard all about it while waiting to pay a cheque in to our local branch of the Midland Bank. I've written about the Marsh branch before, but it is a wonderful place, the only bank I can think of where the staff get excited when you pay money in.

It's about the size of a rabbit hutch but they've just had it refurbished and it looks a treat. They invited a couple of local celebrities to come along and perform the opening ceremony and I must admit that Aileen and I made a very good job of it.

With the advent of rationalization and the birth of telephone banking, the powers that be are closing the smaller branches right, left and centre; either that or they are turning them into electronic bus shelters, just you and a piece of plastic. One day, in about ten years' time, some whizz-kid will have the bright idea that what the public are really after are lots of local branches with real people standing behind the counter – real people who know their customers by name and understand that chanting 'have a nice day' is no substitute for a proper conversation. By which time, of course, all the little local banks will have become video shops or sex shops and I don't think Karen will be there then.

Karen runs the place and she seemed rather quiet

today. She's usually bubbling over, and if her voice isn't echoing all around the walls and bouncing off the ceiling then it's a sure sign that either she's not feeling too well in herself or she's gone home for the day.

I think she was probably wondering where she had gone wrong. How could any self-respecting bank robber go and break into Lloyds when there was a perfectly respectable branch of the Midland Bank over on the other side of the road. They just don't think, these bank robbers.

We had more or less exhausted the subject and I was getting myself ready to launch into a suitably edited version of my adventures with a handbag – you remember, when those six burly men burst through our front door and I held them at bay with just my bare hands and a thorough working knowledge of karate.

I barely had time to open my mouth before an elderly lady tagged on to the end of the queue.

'Did you see that helicopter yesterday?' she chattered on excitedly. 'The one that broke down over Lloyds Bank? Those poor men – they couldn't get down, they were stuck up there for almost an hour.'

I mulled the scene over in my head on the way home. The handsome, square-jawed pilot, his face turning a rather paler shade of grey as he realizes that they have just run out of petrol.

'Never mind number two. Get in touch with the RAC. We'll just have to stay up here until they arrive.'

I told the cats all about it as I humped a huge bag of cat litter up onto the stone table in the cellar. I don't think they ever listen to me. They are too busy finding fault.

'*You've not gone and bought that grey stuff, have you?*'

Thermal jumped up to have a closer look.

'I can't be doing with that grey stuff.'

We hadn't had this brand before, so I cut open the top and peered inside.

'I tried to get those wood chippings, but they hadn't any.'

I bent to have a look at the instructions on the side. You get instructions with everything these days. I read the instructions that came with a loaf of bread the other day. It said to cut it with a knife.

These told me to wear a pair of gloves when dealing with soiled litter and to leave it alone altogether if I was pregnant.

'It's called Sepiolite and it's supposed to control odour.'

Thermal gave me one of his looks.

'What do you mean, control odour? Are you suggesting that . . .'

'No. I'm not suggesting anything. It's just that it smells nice. Here, have a sniff for yourself.'

I held out a handful so that he could dip his nose in it. He was appalled.

'It's that grey stuff.'

'Well yes, but it's a different sort of grey stuff this time.'

'Bet it still scratches my bum.'

'It's only for emergencies and last thing at night.'

He jumped down from the table and stalked off.

'You have an answer for everything, you do.'

Why is cat litter so expensive? Six pounds thirty-five pence for a medium-sized bag of biodegradable gravel. I don't blame the shop particularly, we all have to make a living and it's much the same price at Sainsbury's as it is up at Petals and Paws, but you don't seem to get it any cheaper by buying in bulk and then there's the mental wear and tear of dragging it all the way home, not to mention the hernia.

I wish I had a cat-litter quarry. I could make a fortune. Arthur costs me a fortune all on his own. His litter tray is about the size of Wembley Stadium and he still only manages a direct hit once in every three attempts.

He's never quite got the hang of it. As long as he's got his two front legs buried up to the knuckles in cat litter he assumes that his back end must be in there as well.

I don't like to say anything. I have tried in the past to point out to him the error of his ways, but I wouldn't like to embarrass him.

He's been a good pal, has Arthur, and he has a heart of gold, but he likes to keep himself to himself and he wouldn't know where to put himself if I were to make an example of him in front of the others.

In fact, he can barely manage to clamber in over the side these days and not just because of his illness. It's those back legs of his, he just can't get the leverage. I suppose I could fix a little pair of swing doors for him up at one end, but I bet the lady who owns Petals and Paws will tell me she's just sold out and they don't make them any more.

He did once make a suggestion but I've never taken him up on it.

'*Why don't you spread some on the carpet, right round the edges, then it won't matter if I have an accident every now and then.*'

Thermal and Frink have their trays side by side in the cellar. There, after a long and tiring day, they can chew over the what-might-have-beens and the what-should-have-beens and sort out their tactics for the following day.

Having the trays butted up close together was especially useful when Frink first arrived and was still trying to get the hang of it. She only had to look next door to witness a master in action.

Thermal is the proud owner of a Kitty Corner Cat Pan with its own litter enclosure and it's God help any passing feline who might assume that this was common land. He'd have their guts for garters.

Frink's tray is much smaller. It was once part of a decorating kit, the sort of tray you use in tandem with a paint roller, but it does have its advantages. She's the only one who has a tray with a deep end and a shallow end.

I didn't need to bother with Tigger. She has the exclusive use of a huge meat tray that I found round the back of the butcher's, but I only have to freshen it up every now and then. She has only ever been known to use it on the one occasion. That was when she drank something she shouldn't have from a bucket in a neighbour's back garden and her legs wouldn't work for a while.

She was mortified. I had carried her from the settee where she was recuperating and, as gently as I could, sat her down in the tray.

'*Don't look, then.*'

She tried to cover it up when she had finished but she was too weak to manage and so I did it for her. I think in that moment we bonded in a manner that very few cats and their owners have ever done, before or since.

'*This is very good of you.*'

'Don't mention it.'

There's no rest for the conscientious cat wrangler, you know. No sooner have you dealt with one end of the animal than you have to deal with the other. Lunch for six – the family that eats together, stays together.

Pork pie and pickles for Aileen and myself was the easy part. A glass of wine each and the *Daily Telegraph* crossword and we are as happy as Larry. Aileen closes her eyes and sees each clue in her head as I read them out aloud.

'Ten letters, second letter P . . .'

She usually has the answer long before I do and she can work out fifteen-letter anagrams in her head, which I think is remarkable. She also has the Latin and so I concentrate on the more difficult words such as thrush or knickers and any clue that might require a thorough working knowledge of the game of cricket. Other than that I just read them out and write them down.

Not long ago I sat in a Little Chef with a cup of coffee and the paper, trying to work out one or two answers before I got home so that I could stun her with my brilliance.

At the next table a man wrestled with the *Daily Mail*. He caught my eye and smiled. We crossword addicts are a tight-knit bunch, we have known the pain and we have known the glory. He moved his chair closer.

'Have you been doing 'em for long?'

'I suppose so. Quite a few years now.'

He glanced down at his paper and his eyes glazed over. Then he came out with what I consider to be an extremely profound observation.

'I've only just started recently. Aren't bloody Es useless?'

And he's right. They are. You can get your teeth into a clue if you have already worked out that the third letter is a V or a C. But three Es dotted throughout an eight-letter word will get you absolutely nowhere.

He went back to his paper and shook his head.

'And there's so many of the little buggers an' all.'

So Aileen and I are easy to please, but you can't say the same for the cats. One likes this and another likes that and they can all change their minds in a twinkling of an eye. I sometimes wonder how I manage without a wall chart.

One trick I have up my sleeve is to slip a couple of prawns into whatever it is I am dishing up, and then at least I have the satisfaction of seeing them move the stuff about until they have found them.

I went out into the garden to round them up. We have a sort of tradition that dates back – it must be at least a couple of weeks now. I sit on one of the sleepers and wait and then one by one they come and join me.

We chat about this and we chat about that. Frink always tells me of the great adventure she has just had and how she was lucky to escape with her life. The other three listen patiently and hope that she will eventually grow out of it, preferably by five o'clock this afternoon.

Then, after they have all had their say, we troop back into the house together. It's sort of a family thing.

But today, for the moment, it was just Arthur and me. He lay stretched out by the side of his wire brush and I can say, in all honesty, that his company left a lot to be desired. He twitched occasionally, but that was about as exciting as it got. Then he stirred himself and made for the soft patch of soil under the lilac tree. I was glad he had thought to go before we went in. At least when he performs in the garden you can be pretty well sure he won't miss.

My mother tried to give her cat Whisky the best of both worlds. She dug a large pit in amongst the roses, two feet across and six inches deep, and then she filled it with cat litter.

'But that's supposed to be for inside the house – why can't he just do it on the garden?'

She snorted in disgust.

'How would you like to have to do it on great lumps of wet soil?'

'Well he'll still have to do it on great lumps of wet cat litter, won't he? Once it rains it'll be soaked in no time.'

She didn't deign to answer me, but the next time I called I saw that the litter pit had acquired a pretty thatched roof and I knew I had seen it somewhere before, but I just couldn't place it.

'Where have you got that from?'

'It's off that farmhouse of yours. You never play with it any more.'

I was in my mid-forties at the time and so I suppose she had a point – but all the same it hurt.

Whisky never used it. He always popped round to Mrs Flanagan's next door. But every other cat in the neighbourhood did. It became a meeting place for fine minds. They used to sit there for hours reading the *Daily Mirror*.

'Look,' my mother told me, pointing to the evidence, 'and you said I was being daft.'

There was no way I could prove it wasn't Whisky's, not without taking it for DNA testing, so I let the matter lie – in more ways than one.

I was wondering where on earth the cats could have got to when Thermal came storming up the path, looking so alive that I knew he had been in some kind of a scrape.

'Have you been over to the park again?'

His fur seemed to have a life of its own. It bounced around on his back like an ill-fitting set of loose covers and his pouter pigeon of a chest seemed just about fit to burst.

'*No speaka da English.*'

He never lets on. I would love to know what he gets up to over there.

Tigger arrived a few minutes later, or rather she didn't. She had been with us all along, tucked up in the catmint not more than a yard away. Good job Arthur and I hadn't been talking about her.

We waited for Frink, but there was no sign of her. Aileen came out and whistled and that usually does the trick, although it does grate somewhat. Cats ring up from as far away as Holmfirth to tell her to shut up.

Eventually we drifted into the kitchen. She would be along any minute, she was growing up and finding her feet, but I couldn't help worrying. Three or four times during lunch I went to the back door and called out her name, but I could have been whistling in the wind for all the good it did.

I would just do the washing-up and then have a look round. She never went far. It was a lovely day, maybe she was having too good a time.

That's the trouble with me, I worry too much.

CHAPTER FOURTEEN

The sun was warm on my back as I combed the spare land by the side of the house. My first thought had been the road that runs alongside the park. The traffic whips through at a fair old rate and I had dreaded the idea of finding Frink's little body in the gutter.

We always think the worst, don't we? She had only been missing for an hour or so and already I had that sinking feeling in the pit of my stomach. But from here I could see Bridie O'Connell's house hiding behind the thin trees and bushes and I wondered why I hadn't thought of it before.

Frink and Chico had become firm friends and Bridie often treated the pair of them to elevenses, after which they slept it off, curled up on the hearth in front of a real coal fire. Bridie's meals are substantial to say the least and you need to sleep them off.

I walked up the path and tried the back door. It was locked and I knocked, but there was no-one in. Perhaps she had just popped along to the shops and left the two of them dozing inside.

I peeped in the window but all I could see through the net curtains was a rich warm glow from the fire and enough evidence on the draining-board to show that the idle devil hadn't even bothered to wash the pots before she went out. She hadn't bothered with her dustbin either and I could hear the dustbin lorry in the distance, so I heaved the black plastic sack from her bin and carted it down the path. God knows what she puts in it – she had just had a new sideboard delivered, perhaps the old one was in here.

I went and sat on the stone wall that runs the length of the narrow lane and a couple of magpies came to have a look at me. They've been around for some time now and they really are beautiful birds. They never let one another out of their sight, always bobbing around within a few yards of each other. They seem to be very well matched and I wondered how they would cope if anything untoward ever happened.

As the sun grew in confidence it began poking its nose in under the hedges and then, with a spectacular flourish, it suddenly backlit the ivy growing on the wall behind my garage.

For years I have had a running battle with that ivy; it's tearing the garage apart with its bare hands. I've tried talking to it but you know what ivy's like, it just won't listen to reason, so last year I cut through all the roots at bootlace level and soaked them in some stuff designed to bring an oak tree tumbling down on its knees.

It thrived on it, and perhaps it was just as well it did. An old man who looked as though he knew about such matters told me that the ivy was the only thing holding the wall together, so perhaps those shiny new leaves glinting in the sunlight weren't such a bad thing after all.

Some of the leaves were fresh-faced and healthy and were dressed in a pale Lincoln green, while others were kitted out in a more sombre hue; and then there were the youngsters, still looking a little on the pasty side as they slowly unwrapped themselves and fought for a place in the sun. I was glad it had survived. Ivy and stone always look good together – a pity whoever had tossed that white plastic carrier bag in amongst the roots hadn't appreciated that.

I could hear the dustbin lorry getting nearer, might as well stick it in one of the bin-liners while I was out here.

As I moved in closer I could see that it wasn't a carrier bag at all. It looked just like a lump of moulded polystyrene from out of some carton or other. It was shaped like a small camel, with a hump and a sort of a head and two stumpy legs, and then I pulled up short as my head began to fill with the stone-cold panic that always comes swimming in when you know you are about to see something you don't want to see at all.

It was Frink, and she was lying all bunched up under the wall. I bent and laid my hand on her flank, half hoping she was having me on – she was always playing tricks.

I picked her up and she was warm and soft and she was very, very still. There was a trickle of fresh blood running out of her mouth and down her cheek, just as the wet tears were beginning to run down mine.

Time seemed to stand still. She must have been knocked down by a car. We have half a dozen a day at the very most in this little backwater – how on earth could it have happened?

A voice came from over my shoulder.

'Was it yours?'

'Yes.'

The dustbin lorry had come to a halt just a yard behind me. It was probably quite easy to get knocked down in this lane.

'Do you want me to chuck it in the back of the cart for you?'

'No I don't.'

He turned and walked away.

'I was only asking,' I heard him mutter. 'For God's sake – it's only a bloody cat.'

Another voice, and then a hand that reached out and stroked the kitten's head.

'Don't mind him. You have to understand – we find dozens of them every week, lying in the gutters. You can't take 'em all to heart.'

'No I know. But this one was different.'

He offered me a black plastic bin-liner, sticking it underneath my right arm.

'I know how you feel,' he said. 'I lost my Airedale not long ago. He used to fetch the kids from school for me, all on his own. He made sure they never got bullied while he was around. He got himself run over as well. I backed the car out of the garage, just as he was coming over to say hello to me.'

The lorry lurched off down the narrow lane, its wing mirrors almost clipping the walls on either side. The man nodded towards the garage roof.

'I think you've got company.'

Thermal was staring at the bundle in my arms and

then, as I made a move to leave, he leapt down onto the wall and went to wait for me by the steps.

'I'd better go and break the news to my wife.'

'Yes – that's always the worst part, isn't it?'

'It was her cat really.'

He walked back towards the gate with me and then followed me down the steps. Thermal stalked behind us, keeping a worldly-wise distance between himself and this unknown intruder. What a pity the kitten hadn't had a little more time in which to learn the facts of life. The man turned to leave.

'Thank you,' I said. 'And I'm very sorry about your dog.'

'And I'm sorry about this little one here,' he murmured, gently rubbing his thumb down the length of her back. 'I hope your wife doesn't take it too badly.'

She was heartbroken; she adored Frink. The other three cats come running to me with their problems. I feed them and sort them out at night and generally act as everything from marriage guidance counsellor to father confessor. But they have to be on the lookout whenever Aileen is around. She can't see them unless they happen to be standing on her chest and so she did tend to tread on them rather a lot; and having a stiletto heel stuck in your ribs while you're all stretched out on a shag-pile carpet and dreaming of your early days as a kitten in Brighouse can be very wearing on the nerves.

Falling full-length over a stretched-out cat that you never knew was there isn't all that much fun either, so eventually all the parties concerned sat down together and, during a series of rather complicated negotiations, thrashed out a policy in which a pattern of no-go areas became firmly established.

At first Frink had suffered just as much as the others, perhaps more so because Turkish Van cats start out in life as the most badly behaved kittens on earth. She was a hooligan right from the word go; an ounce and a half of frenzied fur, teeth and claws.

Aileen said she would sort this kitten out once and for all and, with a little help from Arthur, she did just that.

Every time Frink misbehaved Aileen would smack her on the nose and then when the kitten tried to take it out on the rest of the cats, Arthur used to sit on her. If Aileen wasn't around, Arthur used to sit on her while Thermal smacked her on the nose.

Then one day the kitten sat down and had a good long think about this. The prospect of living the rest of her life with a curvature of the spine and a very sore nose featured high on the agenda, and eventually she came to the very sensible conclusion that there might be a far better way of spending her time than this.

From that moment on she became the ideal companion for a blind novelist. Most of the day she would spend her hours wrapped around the back of Aileen's neck like a fur collar.

Every now and then she would take a short break to top up her suntan under the Anglepoise desk lamp and then, after an invigorating session of pitch and putt with one of her favourite paper-clips, she would climb back aboard Aileen's shoulders for another session of literary endeavour.

The two of them were rarely seen apart and it was only during these last few weeks that Frink had begun to explore the frightening world outside the garden gate.

I wrapped her little body in a tea towel and carried her round to the front garden. Aileen didn't want to see her buried and to be honest, neither did I.

I have had a morbid fear of graves and graveyards ever since childhood when my Aunty May used to tell me stories of bodies buried in the cold earth. She would sit on the edge of my bed at night and work through her own fears, not looking at me, but staring off into the far corner of the room as she told me of a grave that filled with water, even as the coffin was being lowered on two stout ropes.

'It never did touch the bottom. It just floated and they had to hold it down with a pole while they chucked the earth back in on the top of it.'

Thermal sat on a flagstone by my side and watched as I dug a small hole by the hedge. I hoped he understood what I was doing and why I was doing it – if not he might never trust me again.

I laid the kitten in the ground and then covered her with soil, stamping it down with my feet. I shuddered as I pressed hard and I felt the old shivers begin to run from the soles of my feet and climb up through the hollow of my spine.

A large moss-covered stone served as a marker so that she wouldn't be disturbed, and then I turned and walked back to the house. Thermal stayed on guard, like one of the lions in Trafalgar Square.

We were going to miss little Frink. We had come to know her well in the short time she had been with us.

'For God's sake – it's only a bloody cat.'

No it wasn't. She was feisty and friendly, bright and intelligent and she had affection oozing out of every paw. We were going to miss her very much indeed.

CHAPTER FIFTEEN

We cleared away her bits and pieces. Frink collected things. She could hear a fresh pack of cigarettes being opened at a hundred paces and every time I drew the cork from a bottle of wine she was in the kitchen and at my feet before I had the corkscrew back in the drawer.

She didn't want to know about the cork, but she loved the gold and silver foil. We would roll it in a ball for her and she would chase it all over the house, picking it up in her mouth and shaking it until its teeth rattled.

She had a shoebox under the hall table, and when the game was over she would drop the little ball in there, along with the dozens of other balls of all shapes and sizes she had played with in her short life.

I pulled the box out from under the table and took it into the kitchen. Aileen opened the fridge door and took out the table-tennis balls. The other cats had lost interest in them. They were all right if you needed a quick fix, but they hadn't the texture say of a ball of wool or a dead mouse; better still, a mouse that was still alive and kicking and able to give them a run for their money. But Frink loved them. She kept goal in the hall doorway, with Aileen doing her level best as the dynamic centre forward.

As a spectacle, however, the game had its drawbacks. If the rampaging forward managed to curl a left footer into the top right-hand corner of the net, then the ball would disappear into the lounge. If the goalkeeper brought off a spectacular save then it would find its way under the hall table or the corner wardrobe. Aileen wouldn't be able to find it and Frink never had the sense to go and fetch it for her.

And so we bought a job lot, a dozen or so, and between them they managed to keep the game going for just that little bit longer. At least a couple in every session would bounce back into Aileen's waiting hands. But eventually even they would decide that they'd had enough of this for a game of soldiers, and then they would run off and join the others in the queue behind the video. Then the cry would ring out.

'Deric!'

And I would pop downstairs and round them all up, minus the odd one or two who had had the wit and intelligence to hide away somewhere fresh and demanding.

One other problem was that Aileen could never find the balls in the first place, just at those crucial moments when Frink was urgently demanding that she come out and play with her and no, not in a minute, right now. Invariably I would be off somewhere, talking at a dinner just north of Carlisle, and so, to make things easier for her, after every game I would pick up the balls and then pop them in the fridge, in those dimples in the door where you normally keep the eggs.

Aileen could always go and put her hands straight on them and it really worked a treat, other than surprising the odd dinner guest who happened to be staying over for breakfast.

I took the box down to the cellar and tucked it away on a shelf. I didn't want to throw it in the dustbin, not right now. I'd take it in stages, leaving that for when the memories weren't quite so raw.

The tea cosy still stood proud on top of the central heating boiler. She had been outgrowing it these past few weeks – she seemed to have shot up – and I'd had to trim the handle hole with a pair of scissors so that she could retain a little dignity as she crawled inside.

She had persevered, even though it must have been rather difficult for her to turn round in the night. One morning I could have sworn she was wearing it. She had her head sticking out through the spout hole as she teetered on the edge of the boiler, contemplating whether or not to jump. As I pushed open the door she turned round to face me, looking for all the world like a tortoise in a padded anorak.

I folded the tea cosy into the box and went back upstairs. Arthur sat staring at the fridge door, half-baked and half-awake and all on his own. I think he must have dropped off to sleep again and only woken seconds before, when he heard me coming up the cellar steps.

'*What is it tonight – is it mince?*'

'I'm not sure, Arthur. Where are the others?'

I should have fed them an hour ago and they don't usually let me off this lightly. They must be out in the courtyard. I opened the kitchen door and shouted and then stood back so as not to get killed in the rush.

'*I just fancy a nice drop of mince.*'

'Yes, all right, Arthur. When I've rounded up Thermal and Tigger.'

There was no sign of them. I combed the first floor and then the second and then I had a rather bizarre thought. I hadn't bothered to look in the front garden. Maybe they were paying their last respects.

I don't usually come up with such daft ideas as that. I know I go on about the cats talking to me and I wouldn't dream of denying that I often talk to them. In fact, come to think of it, only the other day I had discussed with Tigger the possibility of clearing out the cellar and setting up a cat co-operative in order to manufacture a wide range of cat baskets in the shape of huge tea cosies. We had decided that Tigger would be in charge of production and distribution and that Thermal would probably make an excellent sales director. Frink had become computer literate after peering for so long over Aileen's shoulder, so she would have looked after the company accounts, while Arthur would be an absolute natural as the old man who sits in the corner of the office and says that it just isn't the same as it was in the old days. But it was only in fun. I don't really think of them as having human feelings. They are cats, no more and no less, and I am very happy with that, and so are they.

It was just a bit of wishful thinking and you can rest assured that Tigger will have to come up with an absolutely viable business plan before we even consider seeing her bank manager about a loan. And then, of course, there's the question of planning permission.

I found Thermal in the top bathroom. He was practising his origami on the toilet roll and I do wish he wouldn't. It was all over the place. He's been doing this ever since he was a kitten. Whenever things weren't going his way he would set about shredding the nearest toilet roll and it was about time he outgrew it.

I chased him down three flights of stairs and cornered him by the jardinière in the lounge, the one that was very expensive, but doesn't look as though it is. Unlike the other one over there, the one that wasn't very expensive, but looks as though it might be.

'Come on out. That was very expensive.'

'No it wasn't.'

'Yes it was.'

'That was the other one, the one over there.'

I hesitated for a second. I do tend to get them mixed up.

'This one wobbles.'

'Yes, of course. You're quite right, I'm sorry.'

It's very difficult to teach a cat a lesson when you have just been taught a short sharp lesson yourself. It takes all the steam out of it.

'Anyway, come on. It's time for your tea.'

Now we were really speaking the same language. He shot out from behind the jardinière and it wobbled. I reached out and steadied it with my hand. Through the window I saw Tigger in the front garden.

She lay full-length on the pavers. Her chin snuggled in between her two front legs as they stretched out before her, one of her paws brushing the moss-covered stone that I had placed over Frink's grave.

I stood and watched her for a while. When Frink first arrived Tigger had avoided her like the plague. She had no time to waste on badly behaved kids and never hesitated to send her spinning whenever she stepped out of line. But as the months passed by the two of them began to grow closer and Tigger would be forever popping in and out of Aileen's office, just to see how the kitten was getting on.

If she happened to be asleep on the settee, on the desk or on the rug in front of the fire, then Tigger would stretch out beside her and reach out her paw so that it brushed against a tail or an ear or, more often than not, that bit of hair that stuck out on the small of her back. And she would lie there for ages, simply watching her.

Just as she was doing right now, in fact. Of course I could be wrong. Maybe she was merely soaking up the late evening sunshine or perhaps something of great interest was going on, deep down in that crack between the paving-stones.

I know what I prefer to think.

The next morning I slipped out of bed as quietly as I could. The alarm clock had told me in no uncertain terms that it was now 6.28 a.m. and that it was high time I was up and about. Which was a bit much since I don't remember asking it to do any such thing.

The huge digital Big Ben that stands proudly on Aileen's bedside table told me in eight-inch-high figures that it was precisely 6.27 a.m. and that I wasn't to believe a word the alarm clock said.

As I pushed open the kitchen door it was now 6.26 a.m. according to the microwave oven and I had the strange feeling that I was travelling back through time.

The video was adamant, however: it was 6.32 a.m. and the morning was simply flashing by. The cooker demurred. Definitely 6.29 a.m., it said, and what the hell did a smart-arsed little newcomer like the microwave know about anything anyway.

I had to admire the manner in which the microwave oven kept its cool and argued its case. The cooker, it suggested, was always going to be a few minutes fast. It was fan assisted.

I picked up my wrist-watch from the kitchen table and strapped it in place. The little hand stood at six and the big hand at half-past, so I went along with that. After all, the wrist-watch was a recognized specialist in such matters and had little else to think about. His family must have been doing this for generations.

Before she went to bed Aileen had left my birthday card on the kitchen table. I recognized the red envelope from last year and the year before that. It's a lovely black card with a big red heart, surrounded by lots of smaller hearts, and it says she loves me very much.

I didn't open it now, I would do that when she joined me later. She always gets very excited.

'What does it say?'

I shall read the printed words aloud and then the message that she herself had written on the facing page way back in 1987. It always moves her.

'That's lovely, isn't it?'

'It is. It's lovely, darling. Thank you very much.'

And then she will take the envelope away and tuck it in between the appropriate pages of next year's diary, while I stand the card in pride of place on the mantelpiece.

It will stay there for a day or so, after which it will mysteriously disappear until this time next year.

All this has nothing to do with the state of the economy you understand. Aileen picked this one herself and we both agreed, all those years ago, that it was probably the nicest birthday card we had ever come across.

Since then she has needed more and more help, until nowadays she would be relying on the shop assistant to choose a suitable card for me. And so the black card and the red envelope come out year after year – it's become a tradition in our family, a bit like the Christmas tree, and we never get tired of that.

Economics do, however, figure heavily in her choice of presents. Over the past few years she has bought me a personalized number-plate for the car, which cost me a further £150 to have registered and fixed.

Hard on its heels followed a year's membership of a health club and gymnasium which now costs me an arm and a leg every November. Then for our anniversary came the satellite dish and decoder, for the use of which I have to pay Sky Television a tidy £25 a month.

I wondered what she might have bought me for my birthday this year and then I came over all peculiar and had to sit down for a while.

The phone rang a couple of hours later.

'Mr Armitage?'

This person was trying to sell me double glazing – at half-past eight in the morning. I can always tell. They don't know me from Adam and so they call me Mr Armitage. They've looked up Aileen in the phone book.

'I don't want any double glazing, thank you.'

There was a short pause. It throws them off balance.

'I'm not selling double glazing.'

Oh hell. This has happened before. I can be such a know-all at times.

'I'm very sorry.'

'It's all right.'

'I jumped to the wrong conclusion.'

'Really, it doesn't matter.'

'I apologize anyway. What can I do for you?'

'Have you ever thought about a conservatory?'

The phone had woken Aileen, jerking her out of bed and back into the land of the living. She was standing in the kitchen wearing a next-to-nothing nightdress and a bemused expression, both of which suit her extremely well first thing in the morning.

'Happy birthday.'

'Thank you.'

She gave me a kiss and then my card.

'There you are.'

We sat down at the table and she leaned over eagerly as I carefully removed the card from the envelope.

'What does it say?'

I read the printed words aloud and then the message she herself had written on the facing page way back in 1987. It moved her.

'That's lovely, isn't it?'

'It is. It's lovely, darling. Thank you very much.'

I made her toast and coffee and had a cup myself.

'I'll just go and put my card on the mantelpiece.'

'OK.'

It looked a little lonely standing there all on its own, but never mind, the first post was due any minute now, so maybe it would be in good company before much longer.

The toast and coffee had disappeared by the time I returned to the kitchen and so had the red envelope. I poured her another cup and settled down to read out loud to her – today's edited highlights from the *Daily Telegraph*. She butted in.

'Before I forget.'

'Yes?'

'There is a present. They promised they would deliver it before lunch-time.'

'Oh you shouldn't have.'

'Don't be silly.'

'No really. You shouldn't have.'

Later that morning the doorbell rang. The man from Securicor handed over a fair-sized carton with quite a bit of weight about it.

'Sign there.'

'Here?'

'No, there.'

'Sorry.'

'It doesn't matter. I'll see to it. Now if you'll print your name there.'

'Here?'

'No, there.'

'Sorry.'

'Never mind. I'll see to it.'

I handed him back his book.

'I bet it confuses everybody, doesn't it?'

'No. Just you.'

Aileen was just as excited as I was. She had the paper-knife at the ready and I had the carton open in no time.

'Oh that's terrific.'

And it was. A dozen bottles of vintage claret, oak-aged and God knows what. Must have cost five times the price of the stuff I haul home from the super-market every week.

'I'm going to ration it. Save it for special occasions.'

But it seems I don't have to. In the small print, apparently, now that I have taken delivery of the introductory case, I have agreed to buy four more cases every year – in spring, summer, autumn and winter.

But it's the thought that counts, isn't it.

WINTER

CHAPTER SIXTEEN

Christmas was going to be all done and dusted early this year, in plenty of time so that we could sit down and enjoy it. I'd made a list and it's always a start, isn't it.

The cards would be written well in advance, with the food ready in the freezer and the kids' presents all wrapped up in pretty paper by the end of November at the latest. December was going to be a horrendously busy month for both of us, we had to be here, there and everywhere and so inch-perfect planning was to be the order of the day. Starting with the list.

I'm good at lists. Sometimes I use different coloured biros and sometimes I don't. It depends on how I feel. This time I used sheets of colour-coded paper, each of which I slipped into a clear plastic pocket. They looked very smart, but Aileen had her doubts.

'You'll have to take them out every time you want to cross anything off.'

She didn't understand. This wasn't any old list. It was a work of art. Once you start crossing things off it ruins it.

'I shall tick them off. With colour-coded biros. On the outside of the plastic pocket.'

'Oh I see. And then rub them off with your sleeve.'

There's no talking to her when she's in that sort of mood and anyway she was way off the mark. I happened to sit on the pale-pink Christmas card list for the best part of an hour and so rubbed off the ticks with my bottom.

Which was why I was on my way up to the new card shop in Marsh. I had already posted over half of our cards, but now I had no idea who I had posted them to. I could eliminate the overseas contingent – they went off ages ago, and there were certain others that I remembered writing. Some I knew I still had to write and those with addresses to be checked were sweating it out on top of the sideboard. That left us with thirty-nine floaters who might, or might not, be about to receive a Christmas card with love from Aileen and Deric. I decided to double-up and take no chances.

I had stopped to admire the doctor's house when she caught up with me. They'd just had it sandblasted and it looked a treat. She must have slipped out of the surgery round the back and she was with me before I knew she was there.

I don't know her name and it's got to that point where it's too late to ask her. She doesn't know mine either. She calls me Gordon and it's too late to put her right.

'Hello, Gordon.'

'Hello.'

I can tell what she's saying when she comes at me from an angle. It's when we are walking together that her voice disappears and goes on ahead.

She's a tall woman, much taller than I am, but she stoops so badly that I finish up much taller than she is. She's like one of those cherry trees, the sort that they cut up for walking sticks. She goes off at a tangent halfway up her back, and although I was walking beside her, it was the woman who was walking in front of us who got hold of most of the conversation.

I stopped outside the card shop. It's called Don't Forget, which seemed quite appropriate. She swung round to face me and nearly had my eye out with her plastic hood.

'Goodbye then, Gordon.'

'Goodbye. Look after yourself.'

The woman who had been walking in front of us had just gone into the shop, so I followed her in and asked her if she would mind telling me what it was we had just been talking about. Apparently it was nothing much.

Don't Forget is one of those shops where you can't help but browse. I shuffled through the racks for a while, but to be honest I find most Christmas cards intensely boring. The pale attempts at humour rarely succeed and the present-day Christmas provides little inspiration for the artist. A Volvo estate nosing under the porchway of a drive-thru McDonald's is no substitute for an old-fashioned stagecoach, with its four black horses pawing the ground outside a snowbound inn. So it was more or less a case of sifting through the sort of traditional cards that I had already sent last year and the year before that, in fact, ever since I was a kid.

I took a break and wandered off into the back room. Aileen loves to come in here. She loves to touch the fragile fabrics and run her fingers over the smooth surfaces of the *objets d'art* that populate the many shelves and tables, while I steer her round this obstacle course, catching this and missing that, having kittens and breathing a sigh of relief when something or other that looks very expensive has had the common sense to bounce. She has to touch everything.

'What's that?'

'It's Alison's leg.'

Alison wanted to show me something. It was by Des Berry. A nude statue of a woman, sitting on the edge of a shelf with one leg dangling down and the other drawn up to her chin. She was twelve inches tall from her ample bum to the top of her bobbed head. I ran my fingers down her back and then around her waist.

This woman was no supermodel. She had rolls of fat in all those places where rolls of fat do tend to congregate, but she was exceedingly beautiful and her toes and fingers were long and thin and absolutely wonderful. She had no shame, and I wanted to take her home with me straight away. But then I saw the price.

'Tell you what. Show it to Aileen when she comes in. She might buy it for me as a Christmas present.'

Alison paled at the thought of Aileen coming in, but gamely agreed to give it a try. I turned the statue upside down to see if she was complete in every detail. She was, and a large man, who I hadn't noticed before and who was now standing right behind me, gulped loudly in embarrassment and fled back towards the Christmas cards as fast as his legs could carry him.

He was still there a few minutes later and I watched him as he sorted glumly along the shelves. He had the air of a man for whom life has always been a bit of a problem and who could see little or no prospect of its improving all of a sudden. Alison asked if she could help.

'My wife bought some cards off you.'

'Oh yes?'

'And she wants some more just the same.'

I joined in, I love a challenge. But first we needed a little more information.

'What were they like?'

He thought about it for a while. In fact he thought about it for rather a long time.

'Angels. There were lots of angels.'

We found him several angels; some of them were quite angelic, but they were nothing like the angels he had in mind. We needed to pin him down and make him come up with something more specific.

'What were your angels doing?'

He thought about it once again, even longer and harder than before.

'They were just buggering about,' he said. 'The lot of 'em.'

I can't think of a more pleasant way of spending a winter's afternoon than searching for a band of angels who are just buggering about. It's my idea of heaven, but they proved to be elusive little devils.

I came across one who had terminal acne. He was doing a loop the loop high above the stable in Bethlehem and would have been well advised not to give up his day job. And we found several others who were loitering about without any particular intent. In fact angels never seem to do much of anything at all. You never see an angel putting in a damp course or doing a bit of painting and decorating. They might fit in the odd gig here and there, a little light busking perhaps, or maybe play a few requests on the harp, but that's about as far as it seems to go.

I would hate to be an angel when I die. I would be bored to death – it's bad enough being one here, on earth.

Thermal was waiting for me by the front gate. He sits on the high wall, staring out through a hole he's made in the flowering privet and in the summer you can hardly tell he's there at all. But at this time of the year the hedge is as bald as a coot, and so there were no leaves and no flowers, just a mass of twigs and a cat that glowered.

'*I've been worried sick.*'

'I'm sorry. I got caught up.'

I dipped into my carrier bag and pulled out a pound of those biscuity things from Petals and Paws.

'I've brought you a surprise.'

I poked my finger through the side of the polythene bag so that he could have a good sniff. You can buy them in either the fish or the meat flavour. He likes the fish best, so I'd brought him a bag of those.

He jumped down, poked his nose in the hole and breathed in deeply.

'*Didn't they have the meaty ones?*'

'I thought you liked the fish best.'

'*Yes. They're very nice. Just fancied a change, that's all.*'

I stuffed them back in the carrier bag.

'I don't know why I bother.'

'*Well pardon me for breathing.*'

We walked up the path together. Rather stiffly, side by side, or to be more precise, bum by ankle. His bum brushed against my ankle.

'*I'm sorry.*'

'No, please. It was my fault.'

It was almost Christmas for goodness' sake. No time for petty squabbles.

'Tell you what I've got.'

'*What's that?*'

'Come on inside and I'll show you.'

There was a time, a few years ago now, when Thermal's best friend was a sultana. His name was Ralph and the two of them went around everywhere together.

Thermal had found him hiding under the pedal bin one spring morning. The sultana had become separated from his colleagues and he frightened Thermal at first because he was big for a sultana and Thermal had never seen one before.

But in no time at all they became bosom pals. And the good thing about sultanas is that they are easily transportable, so Thermal was able to take him around and about and introduce him to the big wide world outside the kitchen door.

It was a love affair. They used to sit on my desk for hours on end, and when Thermal dropped off to sleep the sultana slept with him, safe under the clasp of a warm and loving paw.

The trouble is, sultanas don't live as long as kittens do and Ralph began to grow more and more wizened as the year unfolded. He was old before his time, and Thermal grew more and more agitated as he began to shrink in size until he looked more like a small black pea than the fruity young buck of his shining youth.

Thermal still loved him dearly, but now he kept losing him. Ralph developed the nasty habit of falling down small cracks, and many's the time I would have to fork him out from under the cooker with a knitting-needle.

Then one day he disappeared altogether and Thermal was distraught. We searched everywhere, we turned the house upside down, but to no avail.

I tried introducing Thermal to other sultanas who had similar interests, but Ralph must have had that certain something that is generally lacking in the modern-day sultana because Thermal just didn't want to know.

It took him ages to get over it. He couldn't pass a likely hiding-place without giving it the once-over and then the twice-over and after a while I found myself doing exactly the same thing. It's amazing that a sultana should have made such a lasting impression on the pair of us.

Thermal became quite depressed and eventually I decided it was time for a spot of counselling. I made enquiries down at the social services in town.

Can you believe it? They didn't want to know. Apparently the death of a kitten's pet sultana rates pretty low in their eyes and is, in fact, one of the few areas these days in which experts are not thick upon the ground. I think it's a damn disgrace.

And so I wasn't expecting love at first sight when I produced the packet of sultanas from the carrier bag. Perhaps, at last, we might find another one who would stand head and shoulders above the rest. Maybe their eyes would meet and in that split second – well, who knows?

Thermal watched closely as I decanted the sultanas onto a large wooden tray. That way they wouldn't be able to accuse me of favouritism. They would all stand an equal chance of making an impression on him.

He was certainly interested. He must have sniffed at each and every one of them, which meant that all those sultanas who didn't get to go to the ball were going to have to go straight into the bin.

Then he suddenly decided he'd had enough and jumped down off the table, but his back legs went from under him, taking the tray and a whole regiment of startled sultanas tumbling down onto the floor. They were all over the place. Some just sat there on the cold vinyl, looking bewildered, while the more alert amongst them made a break for it under the fridge and behind the cooker.

It took me ages to round them all up. That's the trouble with Thermal, he never clears up after himself. I did my best but I couldn't be sure I had accounted for every last one of them. In fact as I tipped my dust-pan, piled high with mucky grey fluff and reluctant sultanas, deep into the bowels of the pedal bin, I could swear I felt a pair of small beady eyes on my back, watching my every move.

'*You bastard.*'

We had quite a few phone calls later that week and a fair number of them touched on the same subject. Paul Wolfenden rang from Matlock.

'Morning, Deric.'

'Morning, Paul.'

'I feel rotten. I've only sent you one Christmas card and I've had three from you already.'

'Well, I'm very fond of you.'

Far more worrying was the early-morning call from South Africa. She was concerned for my well-being.

'I was so sorry to hear about your broken leg.'

So was I. I couldn't remember having broken one.

'Are you able to get around at all?'

'I think . . .'

I could think all I wanted, but I couldn't get a word in edgeways. She told me about the time her husband shattered his kneecap and then went on to tell me all about the ankle she broke whilst jumping off a horse, just outside Pretoria.

'It's over three years ago now and it still isn't right.'

During the next five minutes I heard in graphic detail how it had swollen up like a balloon and how the doctor had said that he had never seen anything quite like it before in his life. This had been some ankle.

'And do you know how they got the swelling down?'

'Bag of frozen peas?'

Of course not. Nothing so mundane. And the more she carried on about this blasted ankle of hers, the more I wished I really had gone and broken my leg. At least I would have had something to talk about.

I began to fantasize, waiting for the moment when she would ask me once more about my dreadful injuries.

My leg would be broken in three places, with complications. Abseiling, that's what I was doing. Down an abandoned quarry, just outside Chapel-en-le-Frith. Had to be carried for three miles. By Sherpas.

But I never got a chance to tell her about it. She rang off just as I was having it amputated, so I went off in search of Aileen to see if she could throw some light on the matter.

She was sitting at her computer when I limped into her study, but we had been tucked up in bed for some time before she came up with the answer.

Christmas for the past year or so has brought with it a rising tide of round robins from people we hardly know, a grim crop of faintly photocopied letters to tell us that little Abigail now has her own pony.

Since I have never laid eyes on this kid, the fact that she has also passed her eleven-plus with flying colours hardly has me jumping up and down in delight.

That lovely warm feeling that always comes trotting along in the wake of a personal letter is completely missing – I'm just one of the crowd. British Gas write to me in much the same way.

And, of course, the parents have to be so even-handed. Abigail passed her eleven-plus and now has her own pony, and then we learn that the eldest son, Grenville, has decided to go backpacking in Peru for a year, before he goes up to Oxford. They all seem to float through life on a cloud of self-fulfilment, and just as I am beginning to resent the mere existence of this bloody family – the wife has taken a part-time job in publishing and the husband has opened yet another branch office, this time in Bratislava – they come to that point in the letter where they have to tell us about their little Norman.

Poor little Norman. He seems to have been left behind in this yuppy rush of life. After much soul-searching we hear that he appears to be rather good with his hands and that he wants to work with animals when he grows up. And right there and then I want to adopt him, sight unseen. I have a feeling that if we leave Norman where he is, he's going to spend the rest of his life mucking out after Abigail's pony.

So this year Aileen decided to write a spoof letter. It would be a chronicle of our own exciting life, packed with all the intimate details of our glamorous world. She remembered one of the opening paragraphs.

'So much has happened this year. In the January sales Deric and I bought each other a set of thermal underwear at a bargain price, and in February we were awfully glad we'd had such foresight. And one of the children rang up.'

I recalled another.

'And it seems that our social life is looking up. Deric has been invited to join the Shell Smartcard set, and the very next day the *Reader's Digest* wrote to inform us that, out of millions, we had been selected to go through to the second round of their Grand Prize Draw! Who knows where this might lead?'

And then Aileen unravelled the mystery of my broken leg.

'April was a bit of an anxious time. I had a disagreeable filling at the dentist's on the Tuesday and then the following morning Deric came home with a broken leg. I told him to apologize and made him take it back.'

It seemed the lady from South Africa had taken us at our word. So what did she make of the final paragraph?

'Owing to our incredibly hectic social whirl we've had to cut down drastically on our Christmas card list this year. However, due to some kind of administrative oversight you seem to have slipped through the net.'

We had a nice long cuddle and then settled down to sleep. Aileen turned over and curved herself down the length of my back, winding her fingers round both of the hairs on my chest. As I sighed I remembered another passage from the letter.

'Sex occurred twice this year, on our respective

birthdays. We did consider indulging once again over the Christmas period, but as Tigger had a bad dose of flu at the time it seemed inappropriate. Anyway, you can have too much of a good thing.'

I turned over to face Aileen and whispered in her ear, 'Merry Christmas, love.'

CHAPTER SEVENTEEN

An ever-increasing stack of presents piled up under the Christmas tree, but the best one of all lay sprawled on the back step, licking the milk from his whiskers. Arthur was still with us, and he rose gingerly to his feet as the postman pushed open the back gate. He might not be in the best of health but he never forgot his manners. The postman bent and patted his head.

'Morning, Arthur.'

'*Morning.*'

'And how are you feeling today?'

By the time his battered old brain had sorted out the right words and begun to put them together into some sort of order, the postman had slipped a pile of mail through the letter-box and was halfway across the courtyard. Arthur made a brave move to follow him, but then decided against it.

From the look on his face it seemed as though the words were backing up behind his eyeballs and the frustration of not being able to use them showed even in the thin little haunches and the swishing tail.

I opened the back door. He could use them on me.

'And how are you feeling today, Arthur?'

He was so glad to be able to get it off his chest. As far as I could make out, his back was a little bit better this morning, but he'd been sick in the night, but not really sick you understand – it could have been fur-balling. He said he'd been a martyr to it ever since he was a kitten.

He could still feel that nasty lump inside, but it was the stiffness and the arthritis that was really giving him gyp. The injections had helped, thank goodness. In fact, since the vet had been and seen to him last Thursday he was nowhere near as tired as he had been the previous week, and that dull pain had almost gone, you know – the nagging pain that had been worrying him all over the weekend.

'Well that's something, isn't it?'

'And I haven't had a spot of trouble with my tooth.'

Arthur's tooth was his pride and joy. His mouth had been in such a state when he first arrived. I thought he was going to have to have his gums removed. But the vet had done a fine job on him and he was now the proud possessor of a single shiny white tooth. It clung like a stalactite, just left of centre and was quite capable of coping with delicacies such as an ounce or two of mince, a nice piece of fish or anything that came sealed in a tin from the supermarket. Those tasty morsels that come already wrapped in fur or feather no longer formed part of his diet and he hardly missed them at all.

He seemed to be shrinking. He had never been a big cat, but he'd always looked it. It was his bearing, I suppose, that and his dignity. Even as a threadbare stray, old before his time, with tattered limbs and evil breath that threatened to strip the pattern from his saucer, he had held himself well.

He had lived out in the courtyard for several months before he decided to join us in the house. By that time I'd had his legs fixed and his mouth sorted out and had him separated from his manhood. The moment he began to trust me it would be time to wrestle him off to the surgery once again, so as his body began to heal, his faith in human nature would take a decided turn for the worse.

I remember being surprised when he lined up alongside the other cats for the first time. He wasn't that much bigger than Thermal and yet as he moved away he seemed to grow in stature – a bit like Charles Bronson.

He looked more like George Burns these days, but for the moment he was contented and as happy as he had ever been. Tigger strolled back from her morning constitutional and sniffed at his nose. She wouldn't have done that before he had his tooth fixed. He seemed pleased to see her and followed her into the house.

Nobody in their right mind would have bet on him still being around after all these months and even fewer that he would go and outlive poor little Frink. I was going to have to watch him even more carefully these next few weeks, to see that he didn't suffer. But for the time being he had the comfort of Aileen's pillow, the large radiator in the hall and his own personal litter tray and it was more than he had ever had. All that and three meals a day. His mother would have been proud of him – he'd turned out to be a winner after all.

Bridie had come over with a box of fresh eggs and was now sitting at the breakfast table with Aileen, finishing off the last of the coffee. Her travelling companion Chico was sitting at her feet, finishing off the last of Arthur's milk. Bridie glanced down at my empty cup.

'I'm not depriving you of yours, am I?'

'Yes, you are.'

'Ah well.'

I fished the coffee grinder out of the cupboard for the second time that morning and went to work on the beans. One third Monsoon, two thirds Kenyan – I don't know much about coffee, but I know what I like.

Bridie lit a cigarette and Chico moved on to the saucer of bacon rinds that I had put on one side for Thermal.

'You've been having bacon, have you?'

'Yes.'

'You want to open the back door, let the smell down the village.'

Bridie has this vast store of colourful sayings that she brought over from Ireland with her some forty-odd years ago and she likes to take them out and give them an airing whenever she can. Her timing is impeccable.

'I didn't go to school, but I met the scholars on their way home.'

I don't understand most of them, but even so they have a rhythm about them that charms the ear and a density that challenges the intellect.

'He's a mean one right enough. He'd mind mice at a crossroads.'

I know. It doesn't make sense to me either, but it described the man we were talking about perfectly.

Chico jumped up onto Bridie's knee to see if there was anything interesting left on the table. He noticed a chunk of marmalade that had made a slight misjudgment earlier on when it went and shot head first off Aileen's slice of toast.

It was now bumming about on the table, looking for something better to do. Chico stuck out a paw and grabbed it. He didn't like it, but he swallowed it all the same and then he looked around to see what else there was.

Bridie grabbed hold of him and unceremoniously dumped him onto the floor.

'He'd eat one more spud than a pig, that he would.'

The Irish may be a dab hand when it comes to plastering words all over the place, but as a race they have never really mastered the art of listening.

Bridie finds it almost impossible to sit quietly by while somebody tells her a story. She darts in and out of the narrative like a comma on legs. The moment I started I knew it was a mistake.

'I was in London the other day . . .'

'Ah well, there you are, you see. You get around all over the place. I don't seem to go anywhere these days. Mind you, Sue and I are off to Stratford a week on Saturday. Do you know Stratford?'

'Yes, quite well. Anyway, I was in London and, as it turned out, I had to stay overnight and . . .'

'Sue and I are staying overnight. Not in Stratford though. At least I don't think so. No that's right. They're putting us up in a hotel in Birmingham.'

'Right. So, because I hadn't planned to stay the night I hadn't anything with me, you know, a suitcase or anything, not even a . . .'

'But then, don't you think people always take twice as much as they're going to need? Especially if you happen to have a car. You just fill up the boot, don't you?

'Now if you're going on the bus and you have to carry it yourself, well now, that's a different matter altogether.'

'That's very true.'

'Anyway. What was it that you wanted to tell me?'

I hadn't the slightest idea. When Bridie machine-guns me like that, my mind goes a complete blank. It's a good job I love her.

I looked over towards Aileen for moral support, but she had enough on her plate at the moment. An indignant Thermal had jumped up onto her lap and was demanding to know who the hell had gone and eaten his sodding bacon.

Chico and I decided to leave them to it. We slipped out, unnoticed, into the hall. Chico went first because he can't stand the sight of blood and I followed hard on his heels because I was a very confused man and needed to be somewhere quiet for a while.

But peace was in short supply. The men from Cable Tel were making a terrible mess of the pavement outside my study. The window-panes rattled with their drilling until eventually the light-bulb in the standard lamp unscrewed itself in despair and fell lifeless down onto the carpet below. It all seemed a hell of a price to pay for the privilege of being able to watch unlimited reruns of *The Avengers* on thirty-seven television channels.

I found sanctuary in Aileen's study. The drills still thumped away in the distance, but in here they made a softer sound, pleasantly punctuated by Arthur's snoring as he lay fast asleep in front of the fire.

Tigger must have brought him up here. He didn't make a habit of climbing the stairs these days. She sat by his side, wide awake as a night nurse, watching the rise and fall of his fur as his lungs pumped up and down in time with his nostrils. Chico was fast asleep on the arm of the settee, with his head hanging down off the end as though all the stuffing had fallen out of his neck. If only I could find Thermal I would have the set.

The fax machine had been very busy. The Bradford Playhouse wondered if we would like to go and see their latest production. There would be a sizable discount, they said, if I could get a party together. It seemed like a good idea so I asked for a show of paws, but there was a decided lack of interest and I put their offer onto one side for the time being.

There followed a yard and a half of this and that, culminating in a message from Henry Margolis. He sent me a big thank-you for the two Christmas cards that he had already received this week and wanted to know if there were any more in the pipeline.

Outside the house the drills stopped drilling and the sudden silence brought Chico bounding to his feet. Arthur opened one eye. And then Thermal raced into the room, carrying something in his mouth. His tail was on red alert and his whole body was alive and throbbing with an urgency that had both Tigger and Chico chasing after him in a blissful state of ignorance. Arthur yawned and opened the other eye.

I caught up with them behind the settee. It was a bit of a squeeze and rather unpleasant, in that I was on my hands and knees, faced with three bare bums that had been parked high in the air while the prettier end of each of the three animals closely examined something very interesting, low down by the skirting-board.

I knew then that I was going to come face to face with a mouse very shortly. It would be a very distressed mouse and this was the one aspect of being a cat owner that I could very well do without.

As I crawled forward on my hands and knees the bums parted and let me through. I could see that Thermal was still in charge of the game. He had his victim trapped up against a castor and there was a gleam in his eye that spelled trouble for the mouse. And for me, if I didn't handle this diplomatically. The other two sloped off, grumbling to themselves.

'*He always has to go and spoil things.*'

The mouse must have slipped under the settee. Thermal had his chin buried in the carpet and his head under the frill. I put my chin on the carpet and buried my head under the frill.

'Where's it gone?'

If he knew he wasn't telling me. Then he flicked his paw and a big fat sultana shot out and hit me smack in the face. Thermal was ecstatic. He did a sort of war dance and then settled down, shielding the sultana between his paws.

It must have escaped my dustpan the other day. He would have found it by the pedal bin, just where he had discovered Ralph the first time round.

I sat and watched him and there was love in his eyes. So much so that I felt I was intruding.

'Sorry. I thought it was a mouse.'

I began to back away, but then he picked up his new friend gently in his mouth and ambled off round the other end of the settee. I followed him, and as he turned the corner he jumped over a half-wrapped parcel that was sticking out from under the coffee-table.

Aileen could have tripped over that, I thought, so I picked it up to put it somewhere safe. As I did so, a foot poked out from between the sheets of tissue-paper and the toes were long and thin and absolutely wonderful.

I sat the statue on the hob by the fireplace, knowing that I shouldn't be doing this. She had one leg dangling down and I supposed the other would be drawn up underneath her chin. I couldn't be absolutely sure because, apart from the leg, she was all wrapped up in tissue-paper.

'That's my Christmas present, Arthur.'

He wasn't the slightest bit interested. Just as he couldn't have cared less when Thermal rolled his sultana across the rug and it came to rest just an inch or so from his chin.

Thermal left it there for a moment. He seemed to be waiting for some comment or other, but Arthur had dropped off to sleep again and the moment was lost.

'It's not his fault, Thermal. He doesn't understand.'

But then I remembered his wire brush and thought that perhaps I had done him an injustice.

From that moment on the sultana rarely left Thermal's side. We called him Ralph junior and the two of them went everywhere together, except when Thermal popped out of the house, in which case he would leave him in the brass ashtray on top of my desk so that I could keep an eye on him.

I started talking to Ralph. He had quite a personality for a sultana and I wondered how I could possibly have overlooked him when I spilled the packet out onto the wooden tray. We had long conversations while Thermal was out foraging in the courtyard and I would ask his opinion on articles I had written.

He liked them all. That's something I admire in a

sultana, it's a sure sign of a fine mind and shows impeccable taste.

I suppose having long conversations with a sultana might be frowned upon in certain circles and considered a sure sign of approaching madness. But I am the only one in my circle and we don't look at it like that.

I must admit, however, that there are times when it worries even me. Only the other day I had driven all the way back from Northampton and as I got out of the car Mrs Bramley and Nellie came past.

Nellie was in one of her moods as usual, but at least Mrs Bramley had her pointing in the right direction. The little dog had taken up crouching now and was busily trying to combine this new-found skill with one of her fearsome scowls. But crouching and scowling at one and the same time proved to be a little too much for her and so, after a while, she gave it up as a bad job and simply sat there on the pavement like a glove puppet with piles.

Mrs Bramley bent to look in the car.

'And how's Aileen?'

'She's not been with me. She stayed at home.'

Mrs Bramley was surprised.

'Oh. I thought I heard you talking to someone.'

We chatted about this and that and then she carried on across the road to the park. I stood by the car for a while, out of respect really, waiting for Nellie to pass by.

She came bumping along eventually, first crouching and then scowling, still a good few yards behind Mrs Bramley, who was halfway across the road by now.

I hurried towards the gate. I didn't want to see the little dog go skidding over the pavement edge and into the gutter. Besides I was embarrassed.

Mrs Bramley had thought she heard me talking to someone. How could I have possibly told her that I was congratulating my trousers on retaining their crease over such a long journey.

'You've done very well. I'm proud of you.'

No I couldn't. Not even to Mrs Bramley.

CHAPTER EIGHTEEN

The spirit of Christmas flowed freely through the town centre. It ebbed every now and then, but with so many people jostling in and out of the shops I suppose it was bound to. It juddered to a grinding halt as the old man stepped out onto the zebra crossing.

He didn't look left and he didn't look right. He'd reached that age when you didn't have to. The little white van was almost upon him when the driver slammed on the brakes, but I don't think the old man even knew that he'd gone to the trouble.

He just kept on walking, if that's the right word for the way his legs were behaving. They were far too polite for their own good. They kept trying to go one in front of the other, but every now and then one of them would stop and wave the other one on.

The driver wound down his window and stared in disbelief as the old man bent double in the middle of the crossing and began to sort out his carrier bag.

'You dozy old bugger.'

The old man looked up, he had heard something. It seemed to be coming from the arcade across the road. He picked up his carrier bag and straightened his back. His legs took a deep breath.

'*After you.*'

'*No please, after you.*'

The driver revved his engine and eased the van forward.

'You dozy old sod.'

The old man paused once more. There was that voice again. He couldn't quite make it out, so he hobbled over to the arcade to investigate.

The van made to turn left along Byram Street. It was a very compact van. One of those cute little numbers that florists seem to go in for a lot these days.

It cut the corner and almost flattened an old lady as she was about to step off the pavement, and I couldn't help smiling as, from low down on the passenger door, the stencilled logo of Age Concern winked up at me as the little van passed on by.

Whenever you go into a jeweller's shop where you have to press a bell so that they can have a good look at you before they let you in, then you can be sure that by the time they let you out again it will have cost you an arm and a leg.

I waltzed into Fillans without a care in the world. They had operated on me last Tuesday afternoon and the bleeding had almost stopped.

It had been one hell of a problem getting Aileen in

there without her knowing what I was up to. Sometimes it can be a doddle: 'Let's pop into Dorothy Perkins, they've got a sale on.' This had been a different matter altogether.

'Let's ring this bell and then run away. Damn it. It's too late, they've seen us.' I didn't think she would have fallen for that, so I had told her I was taking my watch in to be repaired.

'I don't think they do watch repairs.'

'They might. Especially since it's a Longines.'

'It's a fake. Nick bought it for you in Bahrain.'

'He said it was a very good fake. Only an expert would be able to tell.'

The man said he knew nothing about watches but he hoped that I hadn't bought it in good faith because it was definitely a fake and why didn't I try their other shop round the corner. 'You know, the one with all the watches in the window.'

And that might have been that if the young woman who was trying on bracelets up at the other end of the counter hadn't waved her wrist at Aileen and smiled.

'What do you think?'

Aileen does a lot of thinking and she's never been afraid to think for other people. Tray after tray of bracelets passed through her delicate fingers over the next half-hour.

'Try that one. It's as smooth as silk.'

The woman on the other side of the counter joined forces with the two women on this side of the counter, providing expertise that combined well with the gut feelings of one and the fingertips of the other.

'What are those?'

'Amethysts.'

'That's beautiful.'

Aileen laid the piece gently down onto the counter, but every now and then her fingers would stray back to the velvet cloth and she would seek out the gold bracelet with the amethysts and stroke it lovingly.

'How much is it?'

It was far too expensive for the young woman and it made me blink a bit. I bought my first car for less than that and it had two good tyres and you could go all the way to Blackpool in it. You could never rely on it getting you back, but it was very good value for the money all the same.

But the bracelet and Aileen seemed to go so well together. And the one great advantage in having a wife whose sight isn't all that it should be is that you can wave your arms to attract attention, point at something without fear of the gesture being picked up, mouth silently that, no, it's not that one it's the other one, raise your eyebrows and nod your head, slip your credit card across the counter, sign the receipt and arrange to come back on Friday morning for it, by which time they will have fitted a safety chain – all without her noticing a single thing.

And so now I held her present in my hot little hand and, after all is said and done, the expense of a gold and amethyst bracelet is nothing to a man who wears a Longines watch.

Best of all it would come as a complete surprise on Christmas Day. Although past experience has often told me that Aileen is nowhere near as daft as I sometimes seem to think she is.

At a time when every other citizen of Huddersfield would be staggering home with enough groceries to fill one of Pickford's larger pantechnicons, I walked into the house with a packet of frozen rabbit for the cats and a large jar of Kenco instant coffee for Aileen and myself.

For once in my life I had planned ahead. What with six children and four grandchildren between us, plus a wide assortment of husbands, wives, partners and lovers, not to mention the perennial friend of theirs who never has anywhere else to go at Christmas and who will be all alone if we don't take him in, we could be looking at one hell of a houseful during the festive season.

So I had started early this year, and over the past two months I had fully stocked two fridges and two freezers, and down in the basement the cold cellar was looking something like it must have done in the days of yore, with the old stone table barely visible under a mountain of mouth-watering provisions.

And as I stuffed the chunks of rabbit into a pan of boiling water I wondered what the hell I was going to do with it all now that nearly all the kids had rung and, one by one, broken the news that they were making a break with tradition this year and going somewhere else.

The rot began to set in after I rang Sally in Brighton. My granddaughter Katie answered the phone. She's four years old, going on twenty-five, and she has a way with words.

'Who's calling please?'

'It's Grandpa. Grandpa Longden. From Yorkshire.'

I have to spell it out. Brighton is a six-hundred-mile round trip from Huddersfield, so I don't exactly get to see her every other day. Sally does her best to keep me fresh and alive in Katie's memory, but the kid sees me more on video than she does in the flesh and each time we talk I feel I have to ease my way back in so that I don't presume on her good nature.

We talked about her adventures at nursery school and then she told me how she could beat her daddy into a cocked hat at karate. The conversation began to hum along as we touched on the burning issues of the day, such as *The Lion King* and *Pocahontas*, before discussing the many problems facing the construction industry in the mid 1990s, with special reference to Lego.

It was as though the gap that lay between us, both in miles and years, had never even existed and it was nice to know that I hadn't lost my touch with the younger generation.

'Is your mummy in?'

'No. I'm afraid she isn't.'

'Can I speak to your daddy then?'

'Just one moment.'

Then she yelled at the top of her voice, 'Daddy!'

I heard Steve moving in on the phone from some other part of the house.

'Who is it, Katie?'

And I could almost see her shaking her head as she handed him the phone.

'I have no idea at all.'

I ran those words through my head as I pushed the rabbit around with a wooden spoon and for one brief moment I considered joining him in the pan of boiling water. But life must go on and there had been another disappointment before I put the phone down.

Steve had to be on duty all over Christmas, so they would be staying at home. Still, it couldn't be helped, we would have to arrange a get-together early in the new year.

Arthur came in to ask if the rabbit was ready yet.

'I could smell it in the hall.'

I bet they could smell it in Brighton, it gets everywhere. During the war my uncle Jack Sims used to bring us a rabbit once a week. Already peeled but still in one piece, it would lie naked on the pantry shelf and I learned very quickly how to steal jam tarts and mince pies with my eyes shut, so that I wouldn't catch another glimpse of the rabbit before it had been diced and disguised and decently clad in a pastry jacket.

The rabbit's revenge would be to permeate every single room as it simmered on the hob and by the time the smell had cleared a week later, one of its mates would be lying on the slab, ready to start the process all over again.

Jack once brought us a hare instead and I asked my mother what was the difference between the two. She thought long and hard before answering.

'Well, a hare is much bigger you see, and they have longer back legs. They have longer ears as well and very short necks, but a rabbit falls off the bone easier.'

After the war we spent a lot of time up at my Uncle Jack's farm at Wadshelf, just outside Chesterfield. My mother would spend the afternoon chatting to Aunty Madge and I would sit on an old stone wall, watching the rabbits playing in the fields, waiting for them to fall off their bones.

Arthur put his head around the kitchen door once more. Rather than go all the way back to his pillow, which was a good yard and a half away, he had taken to nodding off just round the corner, by the door frame. He would be there for me when I needed him.

'How's it going?'

'I'll call you when it's ready.'

'You wouldn't let me sleep through it, would you?'

'Trust me, Arthur.'

***

It's a wonder the other two weren't here. They must have caught wind of the rabbit by now. I opened the back door to let the smell down the village. That would be enough to bring them scampering back home, even if they were off chasing cars on the M62.

But it didn't. It brought Global, the world's roundest kitten, chugging in like a tugboat through the open back door. I don't know whether Global is his real name or not, but that's what we call him round here. I don't even know where he comes from. Word has it that he lives in a pub somewhere not far away, but that could be just a rumour brought about because he looks like a beer belly on legs.

When I think about it, he's been a kitten for an awfully long time. I must ask him about it sometime.

'What do you do for a living, Global?'

'I'm the only professional kitten in Huddersfield.'

He appears every now and then, rolling remorselessly along, with his head down, studying the ground immediately in front of him, acknowledging neither man nor cat nor Mercedes Benz. Cars don't exist in Global's world. He ploughs across the road and it's up to them either to stop or weave their way around him.

Dogs are even less in evidence. The smaller variety jump to one side when they see him coming and the larger ones, who have more to lose by a show of cowardice, simply stand still and are walked under.

There is something about him that defies description, so don't ask me to tell you what it is. But I can vouch for the fact that when Global walks into your kitchen you feed him. Food is all that matters to him. He doesn't get excited about it, he's a professional after all. He just eats.

I found a half-empty tin of tuna with garlic and

herbs in the fridge and I spooned it out into a saucer. Arthur heard the sound of scraping and peered round the door jamb. He caught sight of Global.

'*Oh, bloody hell.*'

Arthur shivered and pulled his head back out of sight and Global began his demolition job, pushing the saucer round the kitchen floor in front of him as he ate.

He has been genetically engineered for eating out of saucers. Walking as he does, with his head never more than half an inch above ground level, he is perfectly positioned to take advantage of even the most unexpected saucer the moment he comes across it.

The saucer did one complete circuit of the kitchen table, arriving back at the starting point as clean as a whistle. And for once Global had some sort of an expression on his face.

He couldn't quite work it out. There was no doubt that the herbs went well enough with the tuna, and the garlic had come as a pleasant surprise, but that certainly wasn't the aroma that had assailed his nostrils as he walked across the park.

His antennae whirred just the once and immediately took him over towards the cooker where he stood like a little pot pig, his head pressed hard against the glass door, his eyes firmly fixed on the nearest lino tile.

I'd had enough. Entertaining Global is like having the Mafia round for tea. I picked him up and turned him round. I don't think he's real. As my hands slid underneath his fat little belly I half expected to find a couple of Duracell batteries, tucked away in a small compartment.

He doesn't like being picked up. Not that he says anything or does anything about it. He doesn't communicate in the normal way. He employs a brand of body language that is still as a duck pond and yet thick with unspoken expletives.

'That was very rude, Global.'

'*Up yours.*'

The last time I held anything this shape in my hands I was playing football, standing on the touch-line waiting to take a throw-in.

I planted him on the back step and gave his bottom a push. He set off like a small tank, across the courtyard and down the path, without so much as a by your leave.

If he thought he had found a soft touch in me then he had better think again. I had enough on my plate without catering for a cat who thought of me as just another rusty link in his food-chain.

But as I went in to answer the phone I knew full well that the next time he came calling I would find him something or other; I always did. He had an aura about him. I could smell it now, so I gave the kitchen a quick burst with the air freshener before I picked up the receiver.

It was Nick, confirming that he and Lisa were flying off to Bahrain to spend Christmas with her mum and dad. There had been a slight doubt in my son's mind as to whether he could spare the extra time or not, but he had fixed it.

'You don't mind, do you?'

'Course not.'

I envied him the sunshine. They were married in Bahrain and I was his jet-lagged best man, flying there and back in three days flat. My feet hardly touched the floor from the moment I got off the plane and I remember very little of the occasion.

I do remember thinking that they made a lovely

couple. But then my beautiful daughter-in-law could stand next to a sideboard and they would make a lovely couple.

'Have a good time.'

'We will.'

And that just about completed the set. Helen and Craig couldn't get over from Fujairah and David and Brenda would be spending Christmas in Croydon.

Paul and Wendy thought that baby Hanna was too young to travel and had told us that Gracie had decided to go off youth hostelling on her own this year, she was four years old now for goodness' sake and it was time to cut the cord.

Annie and Gordon would be staying with Gordon's parents in Essex and I wondered what on earth that perennial friend of theirs, the one who never has anywhere else to go at Christmas and who would be all alone if somebody didn't take him in, was going to do over the holidays.

Perhaps little Gracie might like a spot of company. He could carry her haversack and keep an eye on Ken and Barbie for her while she was out swinging at discos all night.

Arthur had just about had enough. His saliva glands were awash and beginning to back up on him, so he decided it was time to be firm with me. He limped into the kitchen and fixed me with his special look. The one he saves for best.

'*Have I been dreaming about this rabbit, or what?*'

'I'm sorry, Arthur. It's coming up.'

Anyone who has ever handled a pair of chopsticks will be well aware of how difficult it must be to eat with just the one, and yet Arthur had that tooth flashing in and out of his bowl like a rapier, and he was licking his dish clean before his gravy had even had time to settle.

I put some on one side for the others and gave him his seconds, then went down to the cellar to see what I could do about this food mountain of ours. Maybe Bridie, with her extended family, might like to do a deal.

The first thing I saw as I switched on the light was a cat's face staring at me over the top of a dozen boxes of Marks and Spencer's finest mince pies.

'What on earth are you doing down here?'

Then I saw a tail flick up at the other end of the table, round the back of a wire basket that had followed me home from Sainsbury's one day, even though it shouldn't have done. This was either the biggest cat I had ever seen in my life or there were two of them.

'Come on out, the pair of you.'

First Tigger and then Thermal shuffled out embarrassedly, threading their way through a maze of boxes and bottles and brown-paper bags. You can always tell when a cat is embarrassed, it overdoes the old stretching routine in a vain attempt to appear casual and unconcerned.

Thermal had his foot enmeshed in a string bag of clementines and he dragged them along in his wake. Tigger looked thoroughly miserable. She hates being in the wrong. She squirms inside her fur and it would take an especially hard heart to make her suffer any more than she was doing already.

'You shouldn't be in here.'

'It was that woman. She locked us in.'

'You shouldn't have followed her. You know she can't see you.'

'We're frozen solid.'

Thermal jumped down from the table and the bag of clementines jumped down with him, doubling back and catching him an almighty blow on the side of his head. I grabbed hold of him and began to untangle his foot.

'They smell horrible, these.'

'Serves you right.'

A voice shouted from the floor above and then a wary pair of high-heeled shoes began to pick their way carefully down the stone steps, while the voice continued to chatter into a portable phone.

The cats shot out through the cellar door. She wasn't going to catch them twice in the same day. Thermal popped his head back round the corner. He owed me one. I was the man who had removed the clementines from his paw.

'Run. She'll get you.'

I turned my attention back to the stone table and began an informal inventory. Aileen and I would have to eat our way through seventy-two mince pies, seventy-two sausages, four tins of ham – the list grew longer – six loaves of bread, three Christmas puddings, two pavlovas, three sherry trifles. Good job Marks and Spencer had run out of partridges in pear trees.

Aileen came in, all excited, the phone still glued to her ear.

'Annie's coming for Christmas. Gordon's going to spend a few days with his parents and Annie's coming here. Then they'll meet up in Birmingham afterwards.'

That was wonderful news. Annie's good to have around at any time, but especially so at Christmas.

'And she wants to know if you'll meet her at the station.'

I was completing the inventory in my head. A twenty-pound turkey, three large pork pies and enough assorted nuts to constipate a whole battalion.

'Course I will. And tell her not to eat anything on the train.'

CHAPTER NINETEEN

You will never guess what Aileen bought me for Christmas – not in a million years. I was absolutely astonished and I asked how she could possibly have known and she was delighted because she somehow thought I might have guessed what it was going to be and that would have spoiled it all.

It was that statue, the one Alison showed me in the back of the shop and I couldn't have wished for a nicer present.

I gave her a big kiss and set the statue on the table under the window, with the trailing leg hanging down over the edge. It looked terrific and I told her once again that I was thrilled to bits with it and that I really had no idea.

Then it was my turn to worry as I handed over my much smaller parcel and I could only sit and bite my nails as she tore away at the wrapping-paper. You should have seen her face as she pulled out the velvet-lined box.

The frown that sat tight on her brow as she tried to work out which way up the box was supposed to be was suddenly swept away as she clicked the catch open and her fingers told her that I had bought her the gold and amethyst bracelet from Fillans.

She was absolutely astonished and she asked me how I could possibly have known and I was delighted because I somehow thought she might have guessed what it was going to be and that would have spoiled it all.

She gave me a great big kiss and slipped the bracelet onto her wrist. It looked terrific and she told me once again that she was thrilled to bits with it and that she really had no idea.

I know that love makes the world go round, but it doesn't do any harm if both of you give it a little push every now and then.

We had a lovely Christmas. The phone soon became red hot as the family checked in one by one and it was great because we were able to talk to them for hours on end, but I didn't have to cook for them or go and pick them up from the station.

We slept late in the mornings and we read a lot and watched far too much television. Annie had said that all she wanted to do was to relax and not have to think about anything, so we tried to set her a good example.

The cats had never had it so good. They ate themselves stupid and Arthur developed quite a taste for *pâté de foie gras* and sage and onion stuffing. Aileen thought she would give him a nice surprise and so while he was fast asleep she went out into the court-yard to find his wire brush.

It hadn't wintered all that well. So she had to give it a good scrub and then dry it off before she laid it on his pillow, where he would find it when he woke up.

Thermal showed Ralph junior the Christmas tree. Ralph had never seen one before and he got overexcited and made rather a fool of himself. He hid under the video and Thermal spent half the morning worrying himself sick and feeling very left out of it, especially when Arthur turned over in his sleep and discovered his old friend dozing on his pillow beside him.

I suppose Tigger must have felt left out of it too because she suddenly appeared with a large walnut that she rolled about all over the place. She drove us mad as she rattled it along the skirting-board, flakes of paint scattering on the carpet like dandruff. It wasn't even all that attractive, not even for a walnut. Like the guest at the party who can bring the evening crashing down by just sitting there and looking miserable, the walnut had a sour and surly look about it. It was as though it disapproved of Christmas and, considering what happens to walnuts at Christmas, I suppose it might well have had a point.

Aileen couldn't understand what I was on about.

'What on earth's wrong with it?'

'It looks so miserable.'

'It's just a walnut for goodness' sake.'

It looked more like a little wooden prune, sitting there on the hearthrug. The flickering glow from the fireplace lit it on every side, highlighting its many faces, all of which seemed to disapprove of something or other. One face glowered at the Christmas tree, another at the cards.

It was a bit of a puritan, this walnut. You could tell by the way it curled its lip as it stared up at the mistletoe hanging from the chandelier. It seemed to suggest that we were trivializing this most important of occasions.

'It doesn't seem to think much of our decorations,' I explained. 'It looks a pious little devil to me.'

Aileen yanked Thermal's head out of her gin and tonic.

'That's all we need at Christmas,' she muttered: 'a religious nut.'

Even over the holidays there's always a little work to do. I write a monthly column for *Your Cat* magazine and it was getting close to the deadline. Thermal is usually the star of the piece, but I thought that this month I would give Global an airing, just for a change, so I wrote about the world's roundest kitten and the way he has with a saucer.

How Sue Parslow manages to produce a magazine so fresh and bright and good-looking every month is a mystery to me, but she does, and it's well worth writing the article just to hear the way they answer the phone at the office.

'Good morning. *Your Cat – Your Dog*.'

They are a good-natured bunch and take no umbrage at the many and varied responses.

'Sorry, I must have dialled the wrong number. It was *Your Penguin* I was after.'

No good ringing now, there wouldn't be anyone in the office over the holidays. But then the phone went off at my end, so somebody was up and about early on Boxing Day. Obviously some young and thrusting executive who couldn't bear to take a day off. I was right. It was Thora Hird.

'How are you getting on with this play of mine?'

'Er . . . page a hundred and one, Thora. I've had to put it on one side for the moment.'

There was a pause.

'Well you'd better get cracking again. Can't wait for ever. I'm eighty-four, you know.'

'Tomorrow, I promise.'

'And see that you do. Merry Christmas, love.'

'Merry Christmas, Thora.'

I sat at the table in the window, looking down out of my study at the park. The bandstand was all shuttered up for the winter and the trees were naked as nature intended at this time of the year. The two magpies combed the pavement for titbits and he found a rogue slice of pizza that must have escaped last night, on its way home from the pub. She joined him and they shared it between them. Extra topping by the look of it, so all was well with their world.

A handful of roving seagulls were behaving badly in the middle of the grass arena and the local sparrows looked on in disapproval. They might be able to get away with that sort of behaviour at home in Blackpool, but it doesn't go down too well over here.

And then a couple of small coaches pulled up, right below my window. I can't remember ever having seen a bus tremble with excitement before, but these two were positively crackling with anticipation.

The doors flew open and the seagulls flew off. The magpies stood back and watched as hordes of little people poured out of the coach doors.

'Please God. Don't let them tread on our pizza.'

There were fat ones and there were thin ones, but all of them were small ones. Some were determinedly independent and others clung hard to their teachers' hands, legs and backsides. The ratio of minders to children was very high – these were the sort of kids who needed looking after.

I don't know the words they use to describe such children these days and I don't particularly want to know. They will be stilted and politically correct and recently created by jargonauts who mean well.

These children had problems that would never go away, but they were laughing and tumbling over and getting up again and so bloody eager to get at that flat piece of grass over there that my heart tumbled over with them and then got up again as I watched how they coped with life.

They were wearing football shirts and football shorts over their school shorts and jumpers and one young lad, who was about the size of two young lads stuck together, had a quilted anorak poking out from underneath his Manchester United shirt.

The minders brought out the goalposts. A couple of haversacks up at this end and a crate of soft drinks and a wheelchair down at the other.

The kid in the wheelchair was destined to stare at the heavens for the rest of his life, but there must have been something up there worth looking at because he was whooping and hollering along with the rest of them. I had never seen a human goalpost before.

The children were roughly divided into two teams. In fact, I doubt if any two teams have ever been so roughly divided as were these two. There were twelve on the one side and nineteen on the other.

Then one of the minders produced a football from out of a Tesco carrier bag. He bounced it once, and that was the last I was to see of it for the next five minutes. It was immediately surrounded by twenty-nine frantic little bodies.

Two of the little bodies had decided to take time out. One was having his left leg rubbed by a teacher and the other was sitting on the crate of soft drinks, patting a dog.

At first I assumed that these two would be the goalkeepers, but then I realized that it wasn't going to be that sort of a game.

The twenty-nine charged round the park like a swarm of bees and a small crowd began to form. A very small crowd to be honest, consisting mainly of dog-walkers and their dogs, and they were not too sure where they were supposed to be forming as the two teams had now disappeared round the back of the bandstand.

The crowd held an impromptu meeting and very sensibly decided to take up residence behind one of the goals. A great cheer went up as all twenty-nine players reappeared from behind the bandstand, only for it to fade away again as they vanished down the slope and in amongst the trees.

We waited patiently. The dogs sat down on the frosty grass, prompting me to pull up a chair. It was lonely up here in the grandstand, but at least I had a panoramic view and was the first to catch sight of the two teams as they burst through the bushes.

I don't think the other spectators ever thought that the players might attack the goal from behind, but it proved to be a master-stroke. The crowd scattered and a couple of dogs joined in, one on either side, as all twenty-nine players charged over the goal-line, with the ball somewhere in the middle of the ruck.

After the Cup Final at Wembley the winners set out

on a lap of honour, as the losers troop off the pitch in disgrace.

Not so today. Both teams celebrated in style, to loud applause. Two laps of the pitch, all twenty-nine of them, plus the two substitutes, the two dogs and a teacher pushing the young lad in the wheelchair. He was punching the air in triumph, as well he might. He was one of the finest goalposts I have ever seen in my life.

I tried to work but the sound of laughter continued to drift up from the park and my mind began to drift with it, back to the day when I was a dashing mid-fielder, tasting glory for the very first time, in an under-twelves cup final which took place on a proper pitch with real goalposts, two linesmen and a referee, all three of them kitted out in the official black uni-form. They even had a couple of flags and a whistle.

My dad said he would definitely come and watch me. He never had before and my mother said she would come along with him, just to make sure that he did.

He left at half-time. I watched him leave as I sucked at my slice of orange in the centre circle with the other kids. It had started to rain, so he went and sat in the car half a mile away.

My mother stayed on and got wet for the two of them and before long the pitch turned into a sea of mud, dragging at our little legs and dyeing both teams the same shade of khaki.

But all that was forgotten as we scored the winning goal just a minute from time, and as the referee blew the final whistle all the parents raced over to offer their congratulations.

My mother ploughed through the mud and shot

straight past me. She picked up one of the other kids and gave him a great big hug and swung him round in the air in triumph and then his dad ran onto the pitch and took him off her.

She had gone and given our goalkeeper a great big kiss before I managed to attract her attention and make myself known to her.

'I'm here.'

She lifted me high in the air and told me I was the best player on the pitch. She said she had never taken her eyes off me, not for a single minute, and I think I felt prouder at that moment than I had ever done before in my life.

I handed my medal to my dad as I climbed in the car and he shoved it in a hole in the dashboard and said he would have a look at it when we got home. He said he thought he had a cold coming on and he didn't want to hang about.

I was still sitting in the back of that old Hillman Minx, with my football boots in my hand and my socks stuck to the floor, oozing muddy water all over a copy of last week's *Derbyshire Times*, when the study door burst wide open and Thermal came charging in with Tigger hard on his heels. They can be a real pain in the neck at times.

'What on earth is it now?'

'*It's those magpies again.*'

'And what are they doing this time?'

'*They're sitting on our wall.*'

Well it shouldn't be allowed, should it? You never know where it might end up if you allow a couple of magpies to go around sitting on your wall.

'They aren't doing any harm.'

'*They are. They keep looking at us.*'

That was different then. It's one thing to turn a blind eye and allow them to sit on your wall for a minute or so, but when they start looking at you – well, it's got to be stopped.

The two cats shot out into the hall and then Thermal slammed his brakes on and popped his head back round the door.

'Are you coming then?'

I sighed and followed them out.

I have to admit that they do have a most remarkable sense of direction. The staircase reaches up through the middle of the house, winding round and round, and by the time I have climbed to the second-floor landing I've sometimes lost my bearings completely. I know which room is which but I'm never quite sure what I shall see when I look out of the window. It might be the park or it might be Bridie hanging out her washing across the lane.

The cats have no such problem. Should a squirrel stray over from the park and into our front garden they can keep an eye on it from my study window. Then as it runs up the path they fly down one flight of stairs so that they can keep it under observation from the side window in the lounge.

By the time it reaches the wrought-iron gate they will be staring at it from behind the net curtains in our bedroom and then a second after it's turned the corner into the courtyard they will be perched on the window-sill in the dining-room, waiting for it to appear round the end of the railings.

As it moves over towards the rockery you will find them with both back feet planted firmly in the kitchen sink, front paws pounding the double glazing in some primitive form of communication.

'Bugger off.'

Not today, however. If you want a grandstand view of the top of the courtyard wall then there is only one place to be, and that's sitting on the window-sill in the small bathroom on the second floor.

You have to take care not to sit on the brass ashtray where Deric keeps his bits and pieces or brush your tail up against that cheap glass decanter that Aileen says will come in useful for bath salts one of these days.

But, if you are very careful and have a thorough working knowledge of stained-glass windows, then you can see everything from up here. Frink never came to terms with the stained glass. She would spend ages staring out through the green bits and the yellow bits, but you can only see through the red bits and in the end she would get bored and go and sit on the soap tray, playing with the bubbles while Aileen had a soak in the bath.

But these two know what they are about. Thermal was lying on the sill, on his side, peeping through the red bit in the bottom left-hand corner and Tigger was reared up on her back legs, peeping through the red bit halfway up, the bit that curves into the frame.

Fortunately I am taller than both of them put together, so I was able to peep through the red bit up near the top of the window. It's the biggest bit of all and sometimes, as a special treat, I give Thermal a lift up there so that he can take in this rose-coloured world from a new perspective.

But today it was all mine and as I pressed my nose to the cold glass I could see what looked like a couple of vertically challenged flamingos perched on the courtyard wall, wiping their pizza-stained beaks on the coping-stones.

Magpies look better in black and white. In fact, I think flamingos would look better in black and white. There is no way you can take a bird seriously when it's all dressed up in pink.

Except, of course, when they look at you in the way these two birds were looking at us now. One minute they were unravelling the remains of three different cheeses from around their beaks, shuffling little lumps of salami over to one side, and the next they had fixed us with their four beady eyes.

It was a chilling experience. How they sensed we were there at all was a mystery to me. We were two storeys above them and tucked away behind a barrier of thick bottle-bottom glass. But they did, and those eyes of theirs seemed to bore straight through me, like lasers.

Tigger and I moved away immediately, ashamed of being caught in the act. But Thermal, who has no shame, glared back at them, his little body rumbling with indignation.

'*You see what I mean?*'

'Come away.'

But he wouldn't, and so we made our excuses and left him to it. I went back to my desk and Tigger decided to have another look round for her new-found friend the walnut. The search had kept her occupied for the past twenty-four hours, but I didn't rate her chances too highly. Annie hadn't known about the love affair, so she had cracked it open and eaten it. She had said she thought it was well past its best.

I clicked up the script for the play on the computer. Thora's phone call had made me feel guilty about putting it to one side, and as my thoughts slipped back in time my mother began to walk about in my mind once more.

She stood by the French windows, chatting to a neighbour who had come all the way round the back, having failed to make us hear the front doorbell which my mother had never had connected.

'I can't, I'm afraid. I've got to go into hospital for some tests.'

The neighbour was concerned.

'Oh I am sorry. Will you be going privately?'

'No not this time,' my mother assured her. 'Deric'll be coming with me.'

CHAPTER TWENTY

Arthur couldn't eat his breakfast. He pushed it around his plate a couple of times and then he went away and came back a couple of times, but in the end he decided he just couldn't eat it, so he left it where it was and limped off to his pillow in the hall.

If Thermal ever left his breakfast it was either because he had other things on his mind or he'd gone off tuna for this week only. Arthur never went off anything. Even though he had been ill for some time now he had never gone off his food.

He always finished eating first and then he would hang around, pretending to prink up the odd piece of fur here and there. He would concentrate on his chest. That way he could keep an eye on the other two. If he went prinking underneath or round the back he would have to take his eye off the job in hand and that could lead to missed opportunities.

As one cat finished and then the other, Arthur would move in and mop up the leftovers. When Frink was still with us he would sit tight until her saucer was lowered down from behind the kettle. Sometimes I forgot about Frink's saucer, but Arthur didn't mind. He could wait, he wasn't going anywhere. Not on an empty stomach.

I followed him out into the hall and knelt down beside him. He purred when I stroked his head. Arthur had come to purring rather late in life, there hadn't been much to purr about in his early years. But once he had mastered the art he brought to it a rough and tumble enthusiasm that was more Open University than Oxbridge.

But today he purred on automatic, so gently that it seemed to be coming from deep inside the pillow rather than from Arthur himself. I had kept a close eye on him these past few months and, although he hadn't been well, he had thoroughly enjoyed the long summer sunshine and then, after that, the even more reliable winter warmth of the long radiator in the hall.

He didn't seem to miss the more energetic pursuits that are part and parcel of a cat's life. He had turned the mid-morning nap into an art form and stretched it so that it filled his entire day, with time out for tucking in and the odd trip to his litter tray, a journey which was all of twelve inches.

But now instead of sinking into the pillow so that it became a part of him, he perched uncomfortably on the top as though he wasn't quite sure how to do this. I stroked him once more and then went to ring the vet.

Arthur opened just the one weary eye as Mrs Roger put her bag down beside him and then laid her hand gently on his back. He knew her well by now. She was nice. She wouldn't hurt a fly.

'It's up to you,' she said.

'What do you think?'

'You have to make the decision.'

'He's enjoyed the past few months.'

'He's done much better than I ever thought he would.'

Aileen's eyes were filled with tears. We both knew what had to be done. He had just about had enough.

'Perhaps it's time,' I said.

'I think so,' agreed Mrs Roger.

'All right then.'

Arthur had fallen asleep and didn't see her take the needle from her bag.

'He'll feel a little warm, that's all.'

He wouldn't have worried. He knew about injections, they had kept him going long past his time and he never felt a thing.

'Just a minute or so.'

He never woke up again. Aileen stroked him until he was gone, splashing tears all over him.

'He's been such a good friend.'

I tried to hold my tears in check and failed miserably. Mrs Roger stood back and let us get on with it.

'Would you like me to take him away?'

'Please.'

She packed her ancient bag. It looked as though it might fall apart at any moment.

'Do you have a dustbin liner?'

I searched the cellar for something more appropriate. I didn't want Arthur to leave the house in a black plastic bag, but what containers we had were either too large or too small for him and I couldn't think of anything that might do instead. A dustbin liner it was.

'Here, let me.'

Mrs Roger opened the bag and shook it out and then rolled down the top until she had turned it into a sort of cat basket. It could have been a little inflatable dinghy sitting there on the carpet and it bore no resemblance whatsoever to a black plastic bin liner.

'Thank you. That was very thoughtful.'

I laid him in the bag and Mrs Roger covered him over with the rolled-down top.

'He would have suffered if you had left it any longer.'

Arthur had enormous dignity. It shone through his ragged coat and made good his crippled limbs. Friends invariably remembered him as an extremely handsome cat, which he wasn't at all.

You can't buy what Arthur had, and you can't bottle it either. You have to be born with it and he had died with it still intact.

Thermal hardly left my side all week. He sat on my desk while I worked and perched himself on my knee whenever I took a few minutes off. Tigger immersed herself in her charity work and could often be seen in the park, chatting up the down-and-outs. She specialized in the sort of cats that no other self-respecting cat would be seen dead with and she held mass meetings in the hydrangea bushes.

Her average client would be of a nervous disposition and for ever looking over his shoulder. There would be bits of him missing. Sometimes just the odd lump of fur here and there, but in the more extreme cases it might be an ear, or a couple of teeth, and once there was a huge ginger tom-cat who had only three legs and a stump. She brought him home with her and I tried to catch him, but he still had one leg more than I did and I never got anywhere near.

Not one of these reprobates ever gave her a moment's trouble. Milk-swilling mass mouse-murderers acted like perfect little gentlemen whenever they came face to face with Tigger. She would expect nothing less of them and they seemed to understand that.

They also understood that she was quite capable of flattening each and every last one of them if they cut up rough, and so all was sweetness and light over there in the park. Within a week or so of arriving on our doorstep she had sorted out Denton, the neighbourhood bully, and nowadays he is a much nicer cat, shy and retiring with a nervous twitch.

So I didn't worry about Tigger, but Thermal looked lost. He had spent a lot of time in the front garden after Frink had been killed, sitting on the wall near her grave. But he couldn't understand where Arthur had got to and every so often he would go off on a tour of the house, looking under the bed in the little back bedroom and in many of the other places that Arthur had once made his own.

I wished I could sit him down and talk it through with him, but his attention span wouldn't accommodate such a course of action. Ten seconds and that was your lot, unless food was involved or it had been his idea in the first place.

Ralph junior tried to help out, but he wasn't anywhere near the sultana his predecessor had been and so after one or two abortive attempts he retired from the scene, down a crack in the floorboards behind my desk, where he sat it out for the duration.

I sat down and reread the play. After a short spell away from it I had lost the pace and the rhythm and so I walked around the room, acting it out.

I was impressed. Pretty good stuff this. I read it again, but it didn't work quite as well this time. The third and fourth readings dampened my spirits even further and by the fifth I had come to realize that it was a load of absolute crap.

I told Aileen it was crap and she rapped me firmly over the knuckles with her Biro.

'You always say that.'

'I know, but this time it really is.'

'You always say that as well.'

'I know but this time I really mean it.'

'And you always say that as well.'

'I know but this time . . .'

She threw the Biro at me and it caught me a nasty blow, just under my left nipple. Blind people usually make lousy shots. Just my luck to have married a woman who once won the archery competition at the Buckinghamshire games for the disabled. She won the javelin as well, so I shot out of the door before she remembered she had a brass paper-knife sitting on her desk.

George Kaufman said that plays don't get written, they get rewritten, so I set about rewriting. I tinkered with this and I tinkered with that. Then I thought that I shouldn't have tinkered with this. This didn't need tinkering with. That did though, so I tinkered with that again until I got fed up with tinkering with that and went back to tinkering with this. Aileen came in to see how I was getting on.

'What are you doing?'

'Oh, you know. This and that.'

I had a feeling that the play was becoming a little claustrophobic, with too many indoor scenes and not enough fresh air. I sorted through some old radio scripts for inspiration and began to realize that my mother was hardly ever at home.

The Autumn Club organized a series of day-trips every month which they subsidized by holding a massive jumble sale every fortnight. This suited my mother down to the ground. She could get out and about and still be home in time to give Whisky his supper. They would go to Leeds.

'Whenever you're in Lewis's and you want to go to the toilet, always use those that are marked "Staff" – they aren't so busy and they're ever so clean.'

Harrogate was her favourite watering-hole.

'We queued for almost an hour in Betty's for a cup of tea and a scone – it was wonderful.'

Knaresborough ran it a close second. She had bought her camel suit in Knaresborough and every time she went back she made a point of popping into the shop to tell them how well it had worn.

'It's still as good as new and I've hardly had it off my back.'

The staff were always delighted to hear it – even though the shop was now a ladies' hairdressers and had been for years.

'Probably the same people though,' said my mother.

But Chester won itself an extra-special place in her heart. She went back time and time again and it was there that she once found herself in a quiet church-yard with Nellie Elliot.

Nellie had a thing about gravestones. She would comb them systematically, ever on the lookout for dead

Elliots, and she found quite a few of them in her time.

She would write their names down in a little note-book and she was well into her third volume by the time the Grim Reaper called and took her off to join the club.

My mother much preferred going round British Home Stores because their lampshades were such good value, but she was more than happy to oblige Nellie every now and then.

They were having five minutes one day, sitting on a bench by the church door, when a nice young man walked over towards them.

'Could I have your names please?'

'Mrs Longden,' said my mother.

'Mrs Elliot,' said Nellie.

'And where are you from?'

'Chesterfield,' they told him.

'Thank you,' said the reporter. 'If you would like to go in now, someone will show you to your seats.'

The service took the best part of an hour and was one of the most moving funerals she'd ever attended, my mother told me later.

'Apparently he was very well liked.'

They stayed for a while and mingled with the other mourners, but unfortunately when the lady in black asked them to come back to the house for tea and sandwiches they had to decline.

'We shall have to hurry or we'll miss our bus,' Nellie told her.

The lady was very nice about it and said she was ever so pleased they'd come so far.

'Think nothing of it,' said Nellie, but my mother told me afterwards that if it had been left to her she would have been more than happy to go back for a bite to eat. 'If only to see what the house was like.'

I have often wondered what the widow thought. What if the deceased had been a commercial traveller who frequently had to stay away overnight in Derbyshire?

Then when he dies two unknown women travel all the way from Chesterfield to pay their last respects.

But my mother would have none of it.

'The vicar said he was a wonderful husband and a loving father and he did a lot for the Cubs in Chester. He only wished he'd have known him – but apparently he didn't go to church all that often.'

I couldn't use any of this for the play, but it would be nice to think I might have set the widow's mind at rest.

CHAPTER TWENTY-ONE

I made a cup of tea and lit the first cigarette of the day. It's one of those golden moments in life that non-smokers will never know anything about. I coughed and my eyes watered. They'll never know anything about that either.

I picked up the *Daily Telegraph* and turned to the back page to see if we had come up trumps with the crossword. The day before, as every other day, I had read out the clues in a loud clear voice, Aileen had told me the answers and I had filled them in, in easy-to-read block capitals. I was pleased to see that our combined intellects had triumphed once again.

The front page was all doom and gloom and Princess Diana. She fluttered her charcoal eyes at me. On another page the last pit pony blinked at the light as it was led up to the surface for the first time in years. They could have been sisters.

I have never forgiven Princess Diana for having me beaten up in Dillon's bookshop in Leicester. As I was signing copies of *Diana's Story*, a woman marched in and slapped me, then swept my books from the table.

'That's for ruining people's lives,' she yelled.

It took us some time to work out that she must have thought I was Andrew Morton, signing copies of his book, *Diana – Her Story*.

I rather admired the woman for taking a stand. I just wish she'd thought to have her fingernails cut before she slapped me across the face.

The very next page took me completely by surprise. The headline seemed to leap out at me.

SO FAREWELL THEN, ARTHUR
Today a very elegant cat says goodbye to his adoring public

How nice, I thought. The lad deserved a mention. But then I saw that this cat was white as snow and shown to be dipping a delicate paw into a small tin of cat food, and I read that he had decided to retire after a long and successful career in the advertising industry.

It wasn't our Arthur after all. But what the hell, I thought, and so I clipped the headline and pinned it to the notice-board. Arthur would have liked that. It would serve as his epitaph. He had come a long way in life and only this morning he had received a fan letter from Italy; from Pisa in fact. Most appropriate for a cat who seemed to lean both to the left and to the right at the same time as he took his morning constitutional.

I took another look at the clipping and then pulled out the brightly coloured drawing-pins, replacing them with a couple that had been tucked away in my desk drawer for ages. That was better. Brass fittings. Let's hope it made up for the dustbin liner.

Later that morning I had a phone call from the organizer of a literary festival. I had just finished the screenplay and shut it away in a cupboard. I like to let my work lie fallow for a while and then I can approach it later as a stranger.

Sometimes the stranger can be very cruel and find nothing to like about it at all, but this time I thought he might give me the nod of approval. It's not for me to say, of course, but I thought it was a belter.

I was stretched out in a recliner chair when the phone rang. My first reaction was one of annoyance. Who in their right mind would go and ring me just as I was about to collect my BAFTA award for best screenplay?

I apologized to Joanna Lumley for interrupting her, but she said she quite understood and handed me the phone.

'Mr Longden?'

'Yes.'

He wanted me to talk on the Saturday night, the last night of the festival. Top of the bill I suppose. In my befuddled state I wondered if the media had already spread the news of my award. He began to list the names of the other speakers, my supporting cast.

'P. D. James will be here on the Monday night and after that we've got Melvyn Bragg and Alan Sillitoe, followed by Sara Dunant and then on the Friday evening we're celebrating the works of William Shakespeare, with readings in costume.'

Not a bad line-up that. Shakespeare would probably chicken out as usual, but the others would more than make up for his absence. The man went on.

'The whole week is devoted to the best in British literature and so we thought you might make a nice change.'

I went to find my wellingtons, dragging my ego along behind me as I went.

'Come on now, there's a good boy – and for God's sake cheer up.'

An inch or so of snow had fallen in the courtyard overnight, and although it's often safer to leave our courtyard well alone, a little light shovelling would give me something else to think about besides the screenplay. The BAFTA judges had changed their minds at the last minute and made me give it back. They wrestled me to the floor as I was leaving the stage and prized it from my hand. Joanna Lumley was no help whatsoever.

I have a thing about wellingtons. The first wearing of the winter is a painful business. I found them in the cellar, lying on their sides behind the extending ladder and I needed to know if I had vacant possession or not.

Had anything crawled in there and died? Worse still, had anything crawled in there and had children, done out the little back bedroom as a nursery and converted the loft into an office? Did they have friends staying overnight? I banged them hard on the stone floor and nothing fell out. That didn't mean a thing, they could have tied themselves to the furniture and be hanging on for grim life.

I went and fetched a torch and shone the beam down each in turn. But you can't get it to go round the bend at the bottom and then on into the toe, so that moment when I first dipped my stockinged feet into the unknown was sheer agony.

And even now, as I tramped up the cellar steps, I fancied I could feel something nibbling away at my socks. What nonsense. If there was anything in there it would be riddled with arthritis from the damp by now and almost unable to move.

Thermal hadn't bothered with his wellingtons. He trotted on ahead of me in his bare feet, dotting out a trail of paw prints in the virgin snow, and I stood back and watched him in amazement.

He had four legs and yet he only left two prints and they were both strung out in a straight line, as though he were walking on a tightrope. It's a wonder he didn't fall over.

And then I realized that he always walks like that, but I had never really taken any notice before. He put one foot down where the other had been, just like a supermodel. I wonder if that's why they call it a cat-walk.

We worked as a team. I cleared the courtyard and the steps up to the balcony and Thermal went back into the house and kept my chair warm for me in case I might need it when I finished. He's a very thoughtful cat and I would reward him later by giving him a tin of sardines in tomato sauce for his tea. He can't stand the sight of them.

In the meantime I worked away on the balcony and I was just about to call it a day when Tigger appeared below me with one of her reprobates from the park. He walked alongside her, but not right beside her, just a little to the rear of her, as though he didn't want to push his luck. He was small for a tom-cat and he'd seen better days.

Tigger's fur rippled as she moved ahead of him, her muscles dancing in tune with her stride. But her friend wore a coat that was two sizes too large for him and he seemed to be walking underneath it rather than inside of it, as though he had just slung it over his shoulders on his way out of the house. Tigger was showing him around the garden.

'And this is the courtyard.'

'It's very nice.'

'It can be quite a suntrap in the summer.'

'I can imagine.'

She led him over to the rockery and out of earshot, then wrapped her tail around herself like a fur boa as she sat gracefully in the snow. Her friend plonked himself down beside her, just glad of the chance to take the weight off his feet. They sat there for a while, staring at nothing in particular. It wasn't the best of days for showing someone around the garden, but he seemed to approve, and then they both stood up and made for the cellar steps.

'I'll show you the accommodation.'

This was the moment he had been waiting for. She had probably described it to him over there in the park and he was looking forward to feeling the warmth of the central heating boiler, not to mention the wicker basket with the soft Dunlopillo cushion and the wicker chair with the bit missing in the middle that made it even more comfortable than it ever was before. A small frown appeared from nowhere and settled on his face. How could he possibly afford it?

At that moment the back door opened just a smidgen and Thermal squirted through the gap and out into the courtyard. Aileen slammed the door shut behind him and Tigger's new friend heard the commotion and stood rooted to the spot.

Nobody had told him about this one. It was a much younger cat and looked in excellent condition. Oh hell. It was a tom-cat and it lived here and it was much bigger than he was and it already had him in its sights.

If there is one thing I admire about Thermal it's his manners. He immediately went straight over to introduce himself.

'Good morning. My name's Thermal. I don't believe I've had the pleas . . .'

But the little stray didn't hang about to hear the rest of the sentence. He was off like a rocket and he managed quite well until he had to negotiate the corner by the bottom of the steps. The paving-stones turn into sheets of ice the moment I scrape the snow from them. They needed salting and I hadn't got around to it yet.

He skidded and his steering locked solid. He went over and over, three or four times, before crashing into the sleepers. But he was up again and off down the path before we even had time to blink, his loose little coat trailing behind him, doing its level best to keep up.

Thermal made a half-hearted attempt to follow him, but then decided against it and strolled back up the path.

'He's a bag of nerves, isn't he?'

Tigger gave him a look that would have scrambled his brains if only he had been facing in the right direction.

'Prat.'

I told Aileen about the frightened stray as I cooked up a stir-fry for our lunch. Thermal followed me around

245

the kitchen, acting in the unpaid capacity of spillage inspector. So far he had to deal with two cases: a small chunk of pineapple and a slice of red pepper. It wasn't his day.

'How old would he be?'

'I've no idea. Not as old as he looked, that's for sure.'

Aileen pulled open the fridge door and took out a bottle of white wine. Thermal immediately switched roles to that of unofficial fridge inspector with special responsibility for lamb chops. Aileen shut the door and nearly had his head off.

'He sounds a nice little chap.'

'He was.'

From that moment on I thought of him as the little chap. It suited him. Not quite as cloth-capped as Arthur and nowhere near as worldly-wise, but still very much salt of the earth and pea-and-pie supper. He didn't look as though he'd had too much to laugh about so far in life, but it didn't seem to have soured him and I hoped Tigger would bring him back soon. At least we could give him a meal.

Our meal wasn't bad at all. Sometimes I surprise myself. I have been cooking for years, through two marriages and a childhood, and I still haven't got the hang of it.

My mother was a basic cook in the simple, fundamental sense of the word. Basically she set fire to things and then went to their rescue, always without the slightest regard for her own safety.

As a toddler I only ever sampled her minced beef with mashed potato and her rubber egg and beans with mashed chips. I always had at least two green chips on my plate. None of the other kids I knew ever had green chips and so I considered them to be something of a delicacy and saved them till last.

Still to come was her pork chop with the burned bits cut off, but you needed a full set of teeth before you were allowed to tackle that.

She juggled with this extensive menu right throughout my childhood, breaking with tradition only once a year on Christmas Day, when a rather embarrassed chicken would be placed in the centre of the dining-room table, surrounded by a selection of limp vegetables that had been bobbing about in boiling water since eight o'clock that morning.

I soon learned to grill bacon and sausages, at an age when I shouldn't have been allowed anywhere near the cooker. Then I moved on to gammon with pineapple, which my mother said wasn't natural, and I boiled the runner beans for only five minutes and the new potatoes for twenty, which she said she felt sure wasn't healthy.

But she came with me part of the way, and by the time I left home she had added gammon without pineapple to her repertoire and was thinking seriously about liver without onions.

She kept rigidly to this menu for the next twenty years until my father died, at which point she decided to cut back on the wide variety.

'Well, you don't feel like going to all that trouble when there's only yourself, do you?'

Tigger skipped both lunch and dinner and I assumed she must be involved in a series of lengthy counselling sessions over there in the park. I shouted to her a couple of times, but only succeeded in attracting the attention of a small Yorkshire terrier who was busy watering the trees on the grass verge.

'Sorry. I was calling my cat.'
'That's quite all right.'
'Your trees are coming on nicely.'
'Thank you very much. One does one's best.'

He trotted back across the road and then hesitated, trying to work out where he'd left off before he had been so rudely interrupted. So many trees, so little time . . .

Midnight came and she was still out there. Aileen and I sat at the kitchen table and ate pork pie and crinkle-cut beetroot, washed down with a glass of red wine or two. It's all part of a calorie-controlled diet. We control the calories by eating them. They are extremely dangerous and shouldn't be allowed to run loose.

Thermal dribbled a bemused sultana in and out of the table legs. He'd found it trapped behind my desk and set it free. Ralph junior was very grateful and did his best to look it as he bounced off the fridge door and then slammed into the dishwasher before thudding into the skirting-board, just to the left of the fridge-freezer.

Suddenly the security lights came on in the courtyard, indicating that either a prowler had sneaked in through the back gate or a tortoiseshell cat had jumped down off the far wall.

Tigger stalked onto centre stage and then turned to stare back from whence she had come. Nothing happened for a while and then a pair of black and white paws came over the top of the wall, like a couple of grappling hooks. A pair of black ears appeared briefly and then disappeared again, only to reappear seconds later attached to a small black and white face that seemed to be seriously contemplating the onset of an extremely painful hernia.

I could only imagine the back legs hanging down over the other side, swinging desperately in mid air as they tried to come to grips with an obliging stone or a stray lump of distressed mortar.

Then up he came. With one final effort he dragged first his body and then his coat to the summit and sat there breathing heavily and looking very pleased with himself. If only he'd had a flag with him he would have planted it in between the coping-stones.

The euphoria lasted all of ten seconds, until he saw the size of the drop down to the flower-bed. Why Tigger hadn't brought him in through the bars of the wrought-iron gates I can't imagine.

He sort of fell off. What he lacked in style he more than made up for in his ability to drop like a stone. They say that cats always land on their feet. They don't, you know. Not cats that haven't had a decent meal lately and are too shy and retiring to go knocking on doors.

Tigger went and fetched him out of the flower-bed and together they made their way towards the cellar steps.

'*Are you sure it's all right?*'

'*Course it is. Stop worrying.*'

I nearly fell over Aileen as I darted across the kitchen. She was curled up on the floor, helping a cat who wasn't at all shy look for a sultana who was hell-bent on retiring. He had retired behind the wine rack, but I didn't let on. He looked as though he needed a break.

'Come on. Down to the cellar. I'll give you a running commentary.'

I have fixed a fish-eye spyhole in the cellar door and I can see everything that goes on down there. It's fascinating, especially when Tigger is in her Mother Teresa mode and has arranged one of her at-home nights for poor unfortunates.

We arrived just in time to see her hop in through the cat flap. The little chap wasn't at all sure about this, but after a false start and a few words of encouragement he flopped through after her and sat there on the stone floor, looking around him.

'They're in.'

The little cat walked over to have a look at the boiler he had heard so much about. He peered in through the glass door at the roaring jets while Tigger jumped up onto the top and explained all about heat rising. Aileen wanted to know how I could see them in the dark.

'I put the light on earlier. I thought they might be back.'

It wasn't long before they found the two saucers. Tigger was surprised to see them there and so she walked over to check them out. The little chap sat patiently by her side as she tested the temperature of the milk and tasted the beef and kidney. If I said I could hear his stomach rumbling it would be stretching it a bit, but I could certainly see his body language and it was screaming out loud. Nevertheless he sat and waited, after all he was only a guest. Tigger stretched and moved away. The little chap moved in.

'He's eating now.'

'Eating what?'

'I put some food out.'

Aileen shook her head in amazement. She likes to think she's a hard case but she never fools anyone. Especially not now, with Thermal draped around her neck and with both his back feet stuck in the top pocket of her dressing-gown.

'I hope you remembered to use the best knives and forks.'

We waited until he found the wicker basket with the soft Dunlopillo cushion. I think he'd intended to turn round three times before settling down, but he passed out like a light on the second circuit. Tigger jumped into the wicker chair with the bit missing and mounted guard.

'He's fast asleep.'

'Good. And it's time we were. Busy day tomorrow.'

I couldn't sleep. Aileen lay with her head on my shoulder, half here and half there. We had to be in London in ten hours' time. A celebrity lunch, business in the afternoon, followed by a first night at the theatre and then on to the cast party afterwards. Exciting stuff.

'I'm looking forward to London.'

'Mmmm.'

'But do you know what?'

'Mmmm.'

'It's the little things that make life worthwhile, isn't it?'

'Mmmm.'

'Some people might think them all very boring.'

'Mmmm.'

'But it's the little things that bring the most happiness.'

'Mmmm.'

'The little things in life.'

'Mmmm.'

For a moment I suspected she might not be giving me her full attention, but then she turned and kissed me gently on the cheek.

'I've told you before, love, size isn't everything.'

And with that she settled down to sleep. She means well.